THE ADMINISTRATION'S PLAN TO CLOSE THE GUANTANAMO BAY DETENTION FACILITY: AT WHAT FOREIGN POLICY AND NATIONAL SECURITY COST?

HEARING

BEFORE THE

COMMITTEE ON FOREIGN AFFAIRS
HOUSE OF REPRESENTATIVES

ONE HUNDRED FOURTEENTH CONGRESS

SECOND SESSION

MARCH 23, 2016

Serial No. 114–165

Printed for the use of the Committee on Foreign Affairs

Available via the World Wide Web: http://www.foreignaffairs.house.gov/ or
http://www.gpo.gov/fdsys/

U.S. GOVERNMENT PUBLISHING OFFICE

99–556PDF   WASHINGTON : 2016

For sale by the Superintendent of Documents, U.S. Government Publishing Office
Internet: bookstore.gpo.gov   Phone: toll free (866) 512–1800; DC area (202) 512–1800
Fax: (202) 512–2104   Mail: Stop IDCC, Washington, DC 20402–0001

(II)

CONTENTS

THE ADMINISTRATION'S PLAN TO CLOSE THE GUANTANAMO BAY DETENTION FACILITY: AT WHAT FOREIGN POLICY AND NATIONAL SECURITY COST?

WEDNESDAY, MARCH 23, 2016

House of Representatives,
Committee on Foreign Affairs,
Washington, DC.

The committee met, pursuant to notice, at 9:32 a.m., in room 2172 Rayburn House Office Building, Hon. Edward Royce (chairman of the committee) presiding.

Chairman ROYCE. This committee will come to order.

President Obama's race to empty the Guantanamo Bay detention facility is on. In recent weeks and months, many hardened terrorists have been released. Many of them have been sent abroad, and according to the President's closure plan sent to Congress last month, another 35 are set to be transferred this summer.

Unfortunately, we know many of the recipient countries don't have the desire or commitment or even ability to monitor these dangerous individuals and prevent them from returning to the battlefield. Countries like Ghana and Uruguay aren't typical security and intelligence partners but they are being asked to shoulder a heavy burden and a heavy responsibility. And there are real concerns about the administration setting aside intelligence assessments to deceive countries about the threat posed by the militants they are being asked to take in.

That was certainly a finding of our committee investigation into the release of six detainees to Uruguay in December 2014—and I want to thank Mr. Jeff Duncan of South Carolina, the chairman of our subcommittee that focuses on the Western Hemisphere. The top State Department official overseeing Guantanamo at the time wrote to the President of Uruguay that there was "no information" that these six "were involved in conducting or facilitating terrorist activities against the United States or its partners or allies." No information? They were known to have been hardened al-Qaeda fighters involved in forging documents, trained as suicide bombers, fighting at Tora Bora, committing mayhem, committing murders in Afghanistan.

Although the law clearly states that steps must be taken to "substantially mitigate the risk" of released individuals from again threatening the United States, senior Uruguayan officials asserted before that these six arrived that they would not impose or accept

(1)

any conditions to receive these former detainees. Indeed, these six terrorists were housed just blocks from the U.S. Embassy, without the prior knowledge of U.S. officials and, frankly, were often seen outside of the Embassy.

The administration often talks of detainees ''cleared for release'' as if they are no longer a threat. But just over 30 percent of the detainees that have been released are either confirmed or suspected to have returned to the battlefield. Several of the senior leaders of al-Qaeda in the Arabian Peninsula are alums of Guantanamo.

The administration is emptying Guantanamo with the flimsy claim that it is a terrorist recruiting tool. Let me explain that I don't think that if you're standing in line in Raqqa to recruit into ISIS you say, oh, Guantanamo Bay is going to be closed—no need to enlist here. What Raqqa is about, what ISIS is about is the establishment of the caliphate. That's what's driving recruitment and, frankly, the success of ISIS on the battlefield is driving recruitment.

Closing this detention facility has been opposed by bipartisan majorities in Congress and even members of the President's own cabinet. It is no secret that former Secretary of Defense Hagel was pushed out in part because he was not certifying releases fast enough for the White House.

Yet, President Obama remains determined to push out as many terrorists as he can to other countries. Forty-five or so other ''law of war detainees'' would be moved to U.S. soil. Doing so could open a Pandora's Box of legal issues impairing our antiterrorism efforts.

Fortunately, any effort to bring Guantanamo detainees to U.S. soil would be, according to the Secretary of Defense, against the law and that's also according to the Attorney General. I see no interest in changing that law—certainly not by the American people—and our laws must be honored.

The White House, meanwhile, has no solid plans to detain and interrogate terrorists captured today. That's a problem. Indeed, the administration admits that its proposed domestic Guantanamo would not take in any new terrorists captured on the battlefield. If the administration was spending as much time working to capture and detain ISIS fighters as it was trying to close down this facility at Guantanamo Bay, we would be more secure.

ISIS is continuing to threaten and expand in Libya, Afghanistan, and elsewhere across the globe. Europe is under siege by jihadists. We are under attack. So, unfortunately, we are going to need a detention facility for fanatical terrorists whose processing in the U.S. legal system is unwarranted and simply is not feasible. And we're going to need that for some time to come.

And we'll now go an introduction of our panel. This morning we are pleased to be joined by Special Envoy Lee Wolosky. He's the Special Envoy for Guantanamo Closure at the U.S. Department of State.

Previously, he also served as the Director for Transnational Threats at the National Security Council under President Clinton.

And we also have Special Envoy Paul Lewis for Guantanamo Detention Closure at the U.S. Department of Defense and previously

Mr. Lewis served as both the general counsel and minority general counsel at the House Armed Services Committee.

And we welcome them both to the committee. We appreciate that our two witnesses, along with the intelligence community, have already agreed to meet with the committee in April in closed session on necessary classified issues.

Without objection, the witnesses' full prepared statements will be made part of the record and members here will have 5 calendar days to submit any questions or any statements or extraneous material for the record.

And at this time, I would like to go to Mr. Eliot Engel of New York who is the ranking member of this committee for his opening statement here today.

Mr. ENGEL. Thank you very much, Mr. Chairman, and thank you for calling this hearing. And gentlemen, Mr. Wolosky, Mr. Lewis, welcome to the Foreign Affairs Committee and thank you for your service.

We're reminded again today of the terrible cost of violent extremism. I was just on the floor of the House speaking on a resolution declaring our solidarity with the people of Belgium. That's why I just got here—came here right from the floor.

The dark shadow of a terrorist attack has fallen over another of Europe's great cities, and we're all standing alongside the Belgian people today as they mourn the dead, heal the wounded, rebuild what's been broken, and seek justice.

In these situations it's important to look at what more we can be done to enhance cooperation with our partners to prevent this type of violence.

It's also important to reflect on where our policies have gone astray and maybe made the situation worse. So, it's appropriate today that we're taking a hard look at one of the most troubling and divisive symbols of our counterterrorism effort—the Guantanamo Bay detention facility.

The subtitle of today's hearing is what are the foreign policy and national security costs of closing the Guantanamo facility.

But, as policy makers, legislators, and experts have been saying almost since the facility opened, the better question, perhaps, may be what are the costs of keeping it open.

For starters, the prison's a drain on military resources. It costs nearly $5 million a year to keep a person detained at Guantanamo versus $78,000 a year to hold someone in our most secure Federal prison.

Closing Gitmo and transferring detainees to other secure prisons would free up $85 million a year, resources we could put to better use elsewhere to combat terrorism.

The argument against this goes: We need to spend whatever it costs—these guys are too dangerous to bring here. Let's look at that. Today, 91 detainees remain in Gitmo. Since the prison opened, 644 individuals have been transferred out—144 under President Obama and 500 under President Bush.

As of today, more than a third of the current detainees have been cleared for release after a thorough review process. Under no circumstances will these people be released onto American soil.

Like all the others, they will be transferred directly to other countries. Prior to 2009, more than one in five released detainees returned to the battlefield. But, improved procedures under the Obama administration have nearly eliminated this problem.

If the President's plan to close the Guantanamo detention facility goes forward, only a handful of detainees would ever be brought to the United States and those who are would be held in super max prisons.

They're called super max prisons for a reason. No one has ever escaped from one. And who are some of the current residents of these incredibly secure facilities? Terrorists. Zacarias Moussaoui, who helped plot September 11, 2001—as a New Yorker something that I'll never forget—Richard Reid, the so-called shoe bomber, Dzhokhar Tsarnaev, the Boston Marathon bomber, the four men behind the 1993 World Trade Center bombing, and six terrorists responsible for bombing our Embassies in Kenya and Tanzania. All these men will call ADX Florence in Colorado home for the rest of their days.

For the very few prisoners still in the military commission process, we should try them in Federal court and speed justice for their victims. If there's any doubt whether our justice system can handle the most dangerous terrorists, ask any of the people I just listed.

This isn't a question of what rights Guantanamo detainees should or shouldn't be accorded. It's just a simple fact that the Federal justice system has tried and punished terrorists much more effectively than military commissions.

But beyond the dollars and cents or safety here at home, we need to consider the harm Gitmo has inflicted on our security interests around the world and, just as importantly, on our values.

For terrorists seeking to recruit more fighters into their ranks, the Guantanamo facility is a gift that keeps on giving. This prison has become so infamous and so reviled that our enemies no longer even need to call it by name.

Instead, as we've seen again and again, terrorists flip on a camera so the whole world can see, parade out some innocent prisoner dressed in an orange jumpsuit, and cut off his head or light him on fire.

The orange jumpsuits weren't selected by accident. Everyone knows what they symbolize. This prison has helped strengthen our enemies. It has become a stumbling block in our relationship with coalition partners.

After all, it's not just Americans that ISIS is dressing in those orange jumpsuits and it has created deep division here at home, and that's because Gitmo has long strained some of our country's most important values.

It has become synonymous with torture and indefinite detention. When we were going to school, we learned all about rights and the Constitution. This was never allowed under American law.

I want to quote retired Major General Michael Lehnert, the first commander of the detention facility after 9/11. This is a quote from him. He said:

> "Guantanamo was a mistake. History will reflect that. It was created in the early days as a consequence of fear, anger, and political expediency. It ignored centuries of rule of law and

international agreements. It does not make us safer and it sullies who we are as a nation.''

So I ask unanimous consent that Major General Lehnert's full statement be included in the record.

Chairman ROYCE. Without objection.

Mr. ENGEL. Thank you, Mr. Chairman. Coming back to our question, what are the costs of closing Guantanamo? To me, the answers are clear.

The costs of closing the facility are far, far less than the costs of keeping it open. I'm not alone in this view. President George W. Bush was very clear that he wanted to close Gitmo. John McCain made a campaign promise to do the same.

An overwhelming majority of national security and military experts, including former Secretaries of State and Defense, CIA Directors, National Security Advisors, and Chairmen of the Joint Chiefs of Staff think it should be shuttered.

As I pointed out, the arguments against closing it just don't hold up, and at the end of the day, in my opinion, the only justification for keeping the prison open is fear—fear of violent extremism and fear that our justice system or prison system cannot get the job done despite all the evidence to the contrary. Fear is precisely what our enemies want to instill in us.

I don't want them to win. We shouldn't allow that. We should clean up this stain on America's commitment to justice and democracy. We should take away this propaganda tool for terrorists. We should work to implement the President's plan and shut down this prison.

I look forward to hearing from our witnesses. Everyone who knows me knows that I take a very hard line on this. But I think that we are far better off closing this facility for our interests, no other interests—our American interests—than if we leave it open.

So I look forward to hearing our witnesses. Thank you, Mr. Chairman, and I yield back.

Chairman ROYCE. Thank you, Mr. Engel.

Lee?

STATEMENT OF MR. LEE WOLOSKY, SPECIAL ENVOY FOR GUANTANAMO CLOSURE, U.S. DEPARTMENT OF STATE

Mr. WOLOSKY. Thank you, Mr. Chairman.

Chairman Royce, Ranking Member Engel, distinguished members of the committee, good morning.

I appreciate the opportunity to appear before you this morning to discuss the important matter of closing Guantanamo Bay, Cuba's detention facility.

I'm honored to be joined today by my colleague, Paul Lewis, Special Envoy for Guantanamo Detention Closure at the Department of Defense.

Today I'll describe the rigorous processes that determine whether a detainee should be approved for transfer and the extensive interagency efforts that assure compliance with applicable statutory requirements before each transfer takes place.

At the outset, let me emphasize that President Obama concluded that the continued operation of the Guantanamo detention facility damages our national security for many of the same reasons that led President George W. Bush to the same conclusion.

According to President Bush, by his second term, and I quote, ''The detention facility had become a propaganda tool for our enemies and a distraction for our allies.'' It remained so when President Obama took office and remains so today.

The bipartisan view that Guantanamo should be closed is not limited to Presidents Bush and Obama. Senator John McCain has said that he is in favor of closing Guantanamo.

Likewise, former Secretaries of State Clinton, Rice, Powell, Albright, Christopher, Baker, and Kissinger have all advocated closing Guantanamo.

So too have three former chairmen of the Joint Chiefs of Staff and 42 retired generals and admirals. The list goes on.

In addition to leading Democrats and Republicans, world leaders and international organizations from the Pope to the Organization for American States consistently call on the United States to close Guantanamo.

Today, there are 91 individuals detained at Guantanamo, down from the peak population of 680. All together a total of 779 detainees have passed through Guantanamo and of those 688 have departed.

The vast majority of detainees are transferred out of Guantanamo to other countries. Some 532 were transferred before President Obama took office on January 20th, 2009. Prior to the implementation of rigorous interagency procedures that were implemented by this administration and are described more fully in my written testimony.

My written testimony describes at length the two processes by which this administration has approved detainees for transfer.

What they have in common is rigorous review and analysis of all available information in the possession of the U.S. Government and the unanimous agreement of six agencies and departments before a detainee may be designated as approved for transfer.

After a detainee is approved for transfer, the Department of State leads negotiations with foreign governments about possible transfer. We are joined in our efforts by colleagues from the Department of Defense, Justice, and Homeland Security as well as by those in the intelligence community and on the Joint Staff.

The decision as to whether, when, and where to transfer a detainee is the culmination of a rigorous interagency process similar to the initial decision to approve a detainee for transfer.

This process, including the process by which we negotiate security assurances with our foreign partners is described at length in my written testimony.

I look forward to your questions about it. Once we arrive at a satisfactory security framework with a foreign government, the Secretary of Defense seeks concurrence in a specific transfer from the Secretaries of State and Homeland Security, the Attorney General, the Director of National Intelligence, and the Chairman of the Joint Chiefs of Staff.

Only after he receives the views of those principals and only after he is satisfied that the requirements of the National Defense Authorization Act are satisfied does the Secretary of Defense sign and transmit a certification to the Congress conveying his intent to transfer a Guantanamo detainee.

The rigorous approval and negotiation process I've described has contributed to the dramatic reduction in the confirmed reengagement for detainees transferred during this administration.

Thank you again, ladies and gentlemen of the committee. I greatly appreciate the opportunity to speak before you about this important issue and I look forward to your questions.

[The prepared statement of Mr. Wolosky follows:]

Department of State
Special Envoy for Guantanamo Closure Lee S. Wolosky
Opening Statement
House Foreign Affairs Committee
Hearing on Guantanamo Bay
23 March 2016

I.   Introduction

Chairman Royce, Ranking Member Engel, distinguished Members of the Committee: Good morning. I appreciate you inviting me to appear before this Committee to discuss the important matter of closing the detention facility at Guantanamo Bay, Cuba (GTMO). I am honored to be joined today by my colleague, Paul Lewis, Special Envoy for Guantanamo Detention Closure at the Department of Defense.

As Special Envoy for Guantanamo Closure at the Department of State, I am responsible for all diplomatic issues related to the Administration's policy of closing the detention facility, including negotiating the security and humane treatment assurances for each transfer. My office also plays a leading role in the interagency process to determine whether, when, and where a detainee is transferred, and represents the Department in the periodic review process—known as the Periodic Review Board—for certain detainees who are not currently approved for transfer. In addition, we work closely with our Embassies around the world to follow up on the post-transfer status of former detainees.

Today, I will describe the rigorous processes that determine whether a detainee should be approved for transfer and the extensive interagency efforts to comply with statutory requirements before each transfer. Finally, I will attempt to clear up some common confusion surrounding so-called detainee reengagement.

II.   Closing the detention facility at Guantanamo Bay is a Bipartisan National Security Imperative

Closing the detention facility at Guantanamo Bay is a national security imperative. President Obama has emphasized this point repeatedly—at major addresses at West Point and the National Defense University; in numerous State of the Union addresses; repeatedly in statements made while signing National Defense Authorization Acts; at various press conferences; and, most recently, in announcing the delivery of the Defense Department's GTMO closure plan.

The President concluded that the continued operation of GTMO damages our national security before he took office—and he did so for many of the same reasons that led President George W. Bush to the same conclusion. According to President Bush, by his second term, "the detention facility had become a propaganda tool for our enemies and a distraction for our allies."[1] It remains so today.

---

[1] GEORGE W. BUSH, DECISION POINTS 180 (2010).

World leaders and organizations from the Pope to the Organization for American States consistently call on the United States to close GTMO. Its continued operation is an irritant to our moral leadership and to critical bilateral relationships. President Obama publicly lamented recently that, "[w]hen I talk to other world leaders, they bring up the fact that Guantanamo is not resolved."[2] He went on to note that, "[a]s President, I have spent countless hours dealing with this . . . . Our closest allies have raised it with me continually. They often raise specific cases of detainees repeatedly."[3] I am sure this information comes as no surprise to this Committee.

The bipartisan view that GTMO's continued operation harms national security is not limited to Presidents Obama and Bush. Their conclusion that GTMO must be closed is shared by no less an expert in national security than Senator John McCain who has remarked that he is "in favor of closing Guantanamo because of the image that Guantanamo has in the world, whether it's deserved or not,"[4] as well as my boss and your former colleague, Secretary Kerry. Likewise former Secretaries of State Clinton, Rice, Powell, Albright, Christopher, Baker, and Henry Kissinger[5] have all advocated for closing Guantanamo. Secretaries of Defense Carter, Panetta, and Gates have similarly all advocated for closing the detention facility, as have three former Chairmen of the Joint Chiefs of Staff, and 42 former Generals and Admirals.

III.   Current Population & Review Process

Today, there are 91 individuals detained at GTMO, down from a peak population of 680. Altogether, a total of 779 detainees have passed through Guantanamo and, of those 688 have departed. No detainees have been transferred to Guantanamo since 2008, and the vast majority of detainees transferred out of GTMO to other countries—some 532—were transferred *before* President Obama took office on January 20, 2009.

As you know, one of President Obama's first acts was to order the closure of Guantanamo. What is less well known is that the President also ordered the first ever comprehensive, interagency review of all the 240 detainees then in custody at GTMO.

In 2009-2010, more than 60 career professionals, including intelligence analysts, law enforcement agents, and attorneys, drawn from the Department of Justice, Department of Defense, Department of State, Department of Homeland Security, the Office of the Director of National Intelligence, the Central Intelligence Agency, the Federal Bureau of Investigation, and other agencies within the U.S. government assembled all reasonably available information from across the government relevant to determining the proper disposition of each detainee. The review task force examined this information critically, giving careful consideration to the threat posed by the detainee, the reliability of the underlying information, and the interests of national security. Then, based on the review task force's recommendations, the Departments of Defense,

---

[2] President Barack Obama, Remarks by the President on Plan to Close the Prison at Guantanamo Bay (Feb. 23, 2016), *available at* https://www.whitehouse.gov/the-press-office/2016/02/23/remarks-president-plan-close-prison-guantanamo-bay.

[3] *Id.*

[4] Jacqueline Klimas, *Republicans Offer Obama Path to Close Guantanamo Before Leaving Office*, WASH. TIMES, May 14. 2015.

[5] *Shut Jail, Ex-Diplomats Say: Powell, Kissinger, Albright, Baker and Christopher*, L.A. TIMES, Mar. 28, 2008, at A15.

State, Justice and Homeland Security; the Office of the Director of National Intelligence, and the Joint Chiefs of Staff unanimously determined the appropriate disposition for each detainee: transfer, referral for prosecution, or continued law-of-war detention.[6]

Pursuant to Executive Order 13567, detainees who were not approved for transfer in 2009-2010, and who are not charged by military commission or serving a sentence, are subject to additional review by the Periodic Review Board (PRB). The PRB's mandate is to determine whether a detainee's continued detention is necessary to protect against a continuing significant threat to the security of the United States. Like the earlier review task force, the PRB is composed of senior representatives from the Department of Defense, the Joint Chiefs of Staff, the Department of Justice, the Department of Homeland Security, the Office of the Director of National Intelligence, and the Department of State. Detainees appearing before the PRB are assigned a personal representative and have the opportunity to be represented by private counsel, at no expense to the government. Detainees can provide an oral and written statement, submit evidence, call witnesses, and elect to answer questions from Board members. Only when the PRB arrives at a consensus determination that the continued detention of a detainee is no longer necessary to protect against a continuing significant threat to U.S. security is a detainee approved for transfer.

Detainees who are designated for continued detention by the PRB receive a file review every six months and another full review and hearing every three years. The PRB will convene a full review and hearing following a file review if there is a significant question raised in a file review about whether continued detention remains warranted.

So far, the PRB has conducted hearings for 29 detainees, seven file reviews, and three subsequent full reviews. Of the 29 reviews, 16 detainees were approved for transfer, 12 were disapproved, and one review is still pending. Of those 12, seven have received file reviews, only three of which have resulted in subsequent full reviews. Each of the subsequent reviews yielded a decision to approve the detainee for transfer. This track record demonstrates that the PRB is neither a rubberstamp for release nor one for continued detention.

Of the 91 detainees who remain at GTMO today, 36 are approved for transfer. Of these, 24 were approved by the 2009-2010 review task force and 12 were subsequently approved for transfer through the Periodic Review Board process.

Ten of the other 55 detainees are in some phase of the military commissions criminal justice process—either awaiting a trial or appeal, or serving a sentence.

The remaining 45 are currently designated for continued detention but are eligible for review by the PRBs.

IV.   How We Negotiate Transfers

We have made significant progress in transferring those detainees who are approved for transfer. Since I took office in July 2015, we have transferred 25 detainees to 10 countries. The

---

[6] GUANTANAMO REVIEW TASK FORCE, FINAL REPORT i-ii (2010).

remaining 36 detainees who are currently approved for transfer can, and should, be transferred from Guantanamo as soon as possible and in a manner that protects our national security and is consistent with our long-standing policy on humane treatment.

The decision whether, when, and where to transfer a detainee is the culmination of a rigorous interagency process similar to the initial decision to approve a detainee for transfer. The Department of State leads negotiations with foreign governments about the possible transfer of one or more Guantanamo detainees but we are joined in our efforts by colleagues from the Departments of Defense, Justice, and Homeland Security, as well as those in the intelligence community and on the Joint Staff. Often these negotiations occur in two steps: first, the U.S. government seeks a high-level political commitment that the potential receiving country is willing to resettle or repatriate the detainee or detainees and to impose various security measures intended to substantially mitigate the threat the detainee or detainees may pose after their transfer; second, we engage in working-level meetings with the entities responsible for implementing these measures. While the higher level meetings offer the U.S. government the opportunity to convey our expectations and assesses our potential partner's political will, the working-level meetings offer the opportunity, among other things, to share best practices from previous detainee transfers, and tailor integration and security measures to specific circumstances under consideration.

At the same time, U.S. agencies update the assessment of the potential transferee, drawing upon all reasonably available information on a detainee in possession of the United States. It also develops an assessment of the potential receiving country's capabilities. During this process, we provide our foreign partners with the IC's updated assessment of the detainees under discussion and offer them the opportunity to travel to Guantanamo to interview potential transferees. Throughout all of this, we are working to ensure that we achieve a security framework that, applied to specific individuals under consideration for transfer, satisfies or exceeds the statutory requirements for transfers, including that the receiving government has taken or will take steps to substantially mitigate the threat posed by those individuals.

Once we arrive at a satisfactory security framework, the Secretary of Defense seeks concurrence in the transfer from the Secretaries of State, and Homeland Security, the Attorney General, the Director of National Intelligence, and the Chairman of the Joint Chiefs of Staff. Only after he receives the views of those Principals—and only if he is satisfied that the requirements of the National Defense Authorization Act are satisfied—does the Secretary of Defense sign and transmit a certification to Congress conveying his intent to transfer GTMO detainees.

One challenge we face in our effort to close Guantanamo is the fact that many of the detainees approved for transfer cannot be returned to their home country due to security or humane treatment concerns. As my predecessor Special Envoy Cliff Sloan wrote in *The New York Times*, these individuals may not be the worst of the worst, but rather the detainees at GTMO with the worst luck. Of the 36 detainees currently approved for transfer, 29 are from Yemen. Members of this Committee are aware of the dire security situation in that country. The Administration has not transferred a GTMO detainee to Yemen since 2010, and our focus is on resettling these individuals in third countries. Since January 1, 2015, we have resettled 29 Yemenis to five countries on three continents. It is a testament to our strong standing internationally that numerous countries have been willing to provide homes for those individuals who cannot be returned to their own country and who should not remain at GTMO solely because of their nationality. These countries should be commended for taking this important humanitarian step, and for their contributions to the President's goal of closing GTMO in a secure and responsible manner.

V.   Reengagement

According to the most recent intelligence community report pursuant to Section 307 of the 2012 Intelligence Authorization Act, fewer than five percent of those detainees transferred by this Administration—just seven (one of whom is dead) out of 144—are confirmed of engaging in terrorist or insurgent activity following their release from GTMO.[7] Although we would prefer that no former detainees engage in terrorist or hostile activity following their release, the low rate of reengagement for detainees released since January 20, 2009, is testament to the rigorous, evidence-based, interagency approach this Administration has taken to both approving detainees for transfer and to negotiating and vetting GTMO-detainee transfer frameworks.

VI.   Conclusion

Thank you again, ladies and gentlemen of the Committee. I greatly appreciate the opportunity to speak to you about this important issue. I look forward to your questions.

---

[7] OFFICE OF THE DIRECTOR OF NATIONAL INTELLIGENCE, SUMMARY OF THE REENGAGEMENT OF DETAINEES FORMERLY HELD AT GUANTANAMO BAY, CUBA (March 2016).

Chairman ROYCE. Mr. Lewis.

STATEMENT OF MR. PAUL M. LEWIS, SPECIAL ENVOY FOR GUANTANAMO DETENTION CLOSURE, U.S. DEPARTMENT OF DEFENSE

Mr. LEWIS. Chairman Royce, Ranking Member Engel, distinguished members of the committee, good morning and thank you for the opportunity to testify today.

I'm honored to join my colleague, Lee Wolosky. And Mr. Chairman, I particularly appreciate your continued and sustained interest in this extremely important issue.

At the outset, I want to echo Special Envoy Wolosky's statement and make one fundamental point regarding the detention facility at Guantanamo Bay.

The President and his national security team have determined that closing this detention facility is a bipartisan national security imperative.

The President has repeatedly stated that the continued operation of the detention facility at Guantanamo weakens our national security by damaging our relationships with key allies and partners, draining resources, and providing violent extremists with a propaganda tool.

In January of last year, 42 retired military leaders, all retired general officers or flag officers, wrote the leadership of the Senate Armed Services Committee and forcefully argued for the closure of this facility, stating that the issue of what to do with Guantanamo is not a political issue.

There is near unanimous agreement from our nation's top military, intelligence, and law enforcement leaders that Guantanamo should be closed.

This letter was signed by General Charles C. Krulak, a retired commandant of the Marine Corps, Major General Michael Lehnert, the first commander of the Joint Detention Task Force at Guantanamo, General Joseph Hoar, former commander of U.S. Central Command, General David Maddox, the former commander of the U.S. Army in Europe and many other leaders. Many of these leaders reaffirmed this letter this month.

As Lee noted, in addition, former Chairman of the Joint Chiefs of Staff Admiral Michael Mullen and General Martin Dempsey support Guantanamo closure.

It's the opinion of many others in our military. Envoy Wolosky has noted the bipartisan support for Gitmo closure but I think it's important to highlight this broad conclusion.

This conclusion is shared by two Presidents, four former Secretaries of Defense, eight former Secretaries of State and it demonstrates this bipartisan support at the highest level of our national security leadership.

As Envoy Wolosky noted, in his memoirs President George W. Bush himself concluded that the Guantanamo detention facility was a propaganda tool for our enemies and a distraction for our allies.

The President himself made this statement, and as President Obama recently noted, by 2008 it was widely recognized that this facility needed to close. This was not my opinion. This is the bipartisan support to close it.

As the Special Envoy for Guantanamo Detention Closure, my primary focus is on the transfer process. Sixteen detainees have been transferred to date in 2016. These transfers have reduced the Guantanamo detention facility's population to fewer than 100 for the first time since 2002.

Overall, 27 nations since 2009 have accepted Guantanamo detainees who are not from that prospective country. In addition, 13 other countries or territories have accepted repatriation of their own citizens since 2009.

As with our military leaders, foreign leaders regularly cite the Guantanamo detention facility as an obstacle to counterterrorism efforts.

In my written statement, I cite several statements. Cliff Sloan, Envoy Wolosky's predecessor, noted an example. As a highly ranking security official from one our staunchest allies on counterterrorism once told me, the greatest single action the United States can take to fight terrorism is to close Guantanamo.

And I know highlights by other counterterrorism experts from the previous administration—John Bellinger and Matt Waxman, who both worked for the Department of State—noted, the counterterrorism effects of not closing Gitmo and I describe those in more detail in my opening statement.

Mr. Chairman, I'm also prepared to address the plan to close Guantanamo detention facility. The President, announcing the plan, stated that it has four main elements.

We'll continue to transfer, we'll accelerate the POB process, we'll look for individual dispositions and, most importantly, we'll work with Congress to find a location to transfer everybody from Guantanamo safely and securely.

As far as the transfer process, I just want to state that Secretary Carter has forcefully stated that safety is his number-one priority.

He does not transfer a detainee unless he is confident that the threat is substantially mitigated and it's in the national security interests of the United States.

Finally, I'd like to take a moment to recognize the military service members conducting detention operations at Guantanamo Bay. Too often in the course of considering the future of this facility we lose sight of the remarkable men and women who serve honourably under extraordinarily difficult conditions.

They have our deepest appreciation for their service and their professionalism, which they display each and every day on behalf of our nation.

Gentlemen, President Bush worked toward closing Guantanamo. Many officials in his administration worked hard toward that objective. We're closer to it than many people realize.

Of the nearly 800 detainees who have been held at Guantanamo since the facility opened over 85 percent have been transferred, including more than 500 that were transferred by the previous administration.

The President, his national security experts, and this administration believe it should be closed. The senior military leaders of this country and the leaders of the Department of Defense concur.

As indicated in the letter by the retired military leaders, many believe that closure of this facility is the single most important counterterrorism effort the United States can undertake.

We believe the issue is not whether to close the Guantanamo detention facility—it's how to do it. Thank you, and I look forward to your questions.

[The prepared statement of Mr. Lewis follows:]

STATEMENT OF

PAUL M. LEWIS

SPECIAL ENVOY FOR GUANTANAMO DETENTION CLOSURE
U.S. DEPARTMENT OF DEFENSE

BEFORE THE HOUSE COMMITTEE ON FOREIGN AFFAIRS
MARCH 23, 2016

Chairman Royce, Ranking Member Engel, distinguished members of the committee, thank you for the opportunity testify today regarding the Administration's plan to close the Guantanamo Bay detention facility.

I am pleased to be joining my colleague Lee Wolosky, the Department of State Special Envoy for Guantanamo Detention Closure.

Mr. Chairman, I particularly appreciate your continued and sustained interest in this extremely important issue. I appreciate the opportunity we have had to regularly brief you and your staff.

Overview

On January 22, 2009, President Obama signed Executive Order 13492, which ordered the closure of the detention facilities at the Guantanamo Bay Naval Base in Cuba. Pursuant to that order, a special task force was established to comprehensively review information in the possession of the U.S. Government about the detainees, and to assess appropriate disposition options. Through that rigorous interagency effort, the review participants determined appropriate dispositions for all 240 detainees subject to the review, including designation for transfer, referral for prosecution, or continued law of war detention.

Since then, pursuant to Executive Order 13567, signed on March 7, 2011, and consistent with section 1023 of the National Defense Authorization Act (NDAA) for FY 2012, the Periodic Review Board (PRB) has been reviewing the status of those detainees not currently eligible for transfer and not subject to military commissions.

There are **91** detainees remaining at the Guantanamo Bay detention facility. Of these, **36** are currently eligible for transfer, **10** are being prosecuted or have been sentenced, and **45** are in the process of being reviewed by the PRB.

We are making much progress. Secretary of Defense Carter has approved the transfer of **31** detainees – **16** of whom have been transferred this year. Secretary Hagel transferred **44**, Secretary Panetta **4**, and Secretary Gates **68**. During this Administration **147** detainees have been transferred. I note that most of the detainees transferred from Guantanamo were transferred by the Bush Administration, which transferred more than **500** detainees. To date, more than 85% of the detainees once held at Guantanamo have been transferred.

Closure Is a National Security Imperative

At the outset I want to make one fundamental point regarding the detention facility at Guantanamo Bay. The President and his national security team have determined that closing this detention facility is a national security imperative. The President and the leadership of his national security team believe that the continued operation of the detention facility at Guantanamo weakens our national security by damaging our relationships with key allies and partners, draining resources, and providing violent extremists with a propaganda tool.

In January of last year, **42** retired military leaders - all retired general officers or flag officers - wrote the leadership of the Senate Armed Services Committee and forcefully argued for the closure of the Guantanamo detention facility, stating "[T]he issue of what to do with Guantanamo is not a political issue. There is near unanimous agreement from our nation's top military, intelligence, and law enforcement leaders that

Guantanamo should be closed." This letter was signed by General Charles C. Krulak, a retired Commandant of the Marine Corps, Major General Michael R. Lehnert, the first commander of the joint detention task force at Guantanamo, General Joseph Hoar, the former commander of U.S. Central Command, General David M. Maddox, the former commander of the U.S. Army in Europe, and many other retired senior military leaders.

In addition, former chairmen of the Joint Chiefs of Staff, Admiral Michael Mullen and General Martin Dempsey, support Guantanamo closure. It is the opinion of many others in our military.

Senior civilian figures across the political spectrum have also made clear that Guantanamo poses profound risks to our national security and should be closed. This conclusion, shared by two Presidents, four former Secretaries of Defense, and eight former Secretaries of State demonstrates bipartisan support for Guantanamo closure at the highest level of our national security leadership. Five former Secretaries of State-Henry Kissinger, James Baker, Warren Christopher, Madeleine Albright and Colin Powell--- stated in March 2007 that if the next President moved quickly to close the Guantanamo detention facility it would improve our reputation around the world immediately. Former Secretary Powell forcefully reiterated his support for Guantanamo detention closure as recently as last month.

Finally, in his memoirs, President George W. Bush concluded that the Guantanamo detention facility was "a propaganda tool for our enemies and a distraction for our allies." As President Obama noted, by 2008 it was "widely recognized that this facility needed to close. This was not just my opinion...there was bipartisan support to close it," including Senator John McCain, the Republican nominee for President.

Recent Transfer Decisions

As the Special Envoy for Guantanamo Detention Closure, my primary focus is on the transfer process. Sixteen detainees have been transferred to date in 2016. These transfers reduced the Guantanamo detention facility's population to fewer than 100 for the first time since 2002. 2016 transfers include resettlements to Ghana, Oman, Bosnia, and Montenegro and repatriations to Kuwait and Saudi Arabia.

Overall, 27 nations since 2009 have accepted Guantanamo detainees who are not from each respective country. The list is impressive: Albania (3 detainees), Belgium (1), Bermuda (4), Bosnia (1), Bulgaria (1), Capo Verde (1), El Salvador (2), Estonia (1), France (2), Georgia (6), Germany (2), Ghana (2), Hungary (1), Ireland (2), Italy (2), Kazakhstan (5), Latvia (1), Montenegro (1), Oman (20), Palau (6), Portugal (2), Qatar (5), Slovakia (8), Spain (3), Switzerland (3), Uruguay (6), and the United Arab Emirates (5). And Special Envoy Wolosky and I can tell you, we anticipate more countries in the near future.

Thirteen countries or territories have accepted repatriations of their own citizens since 2009: Afghanistan (9), Algeria (9), Canada (1), Chad (1), Iraq (1), Kuwait (4), Morocco (1), Mauritania (1), Saudi Arabia (8), Somaliland (2), Sudan (3), United Kingdom (2), and Yemen (8). This list is also impressive and demonstrates the broad support in the international community for closure.

This broad support in the international community is also demonstrated by the numerous international organizations calling for closure, including the Organization of American States and the Roman Catholic Church.

As with our military leaders, foreign leaders regularly cite the Guantanamo detention center as an obstacle to counterterrorism efforts. Let me give you several examples that highlight this important point.

Cliff Sloan, the former Department of State Special Envoy, frequently recalled strong language from our allies similar to the letter from the retired military leaders. Sloan stated as an example: "[A]s a high-ranking security official from one of our staunchest allies on counterterrorism (not from Europe) once told me, 'The greatest single action the United States can take to fight terrorism is to close Guantánamo.'"

When we assess the foreign policy and national security costs of this facility, the data highlighted above, stands out to me. Twenty-seven countries are asking us, if they can safely and responsibly take Guantanamo detainees, "Why can't the United States?"

President Obama highlighted this continuing issue in his statement on closing the facility on February 23, 2016. The President directly addressed the high cost of Guantanamo to our foreign policy aims, indicating that foreign leaders continuously bring up the topic of Guantanamo closure and specific detainees repeatedly during his leadership meetings with them.

Leaders of the Bush Administration reached the same conclusion. President Bush himself, as indicated above, referenced the "distraction" with our allies that Guantanamo cost us during his Presidency.

John Bellinger, the former Legal Advisor to the National Security Council and the Department of State during the previous Administration, stated at a Brookings Institution event in January 2010: "[O]n balance, Guantanamo does the American people more harm than good." He emphasized that this detention facility "undermines vital counterterrorism cooperation from our Western allies, who view the prison as inconsistent with their own and U.S. values. It has proved impossible to shake these unfair perceptions." Mr. Bellinger summarizes this issue well.

Professor Matt Waxman, the first Deputy Assistant Secretary of Defense for Detainee Affairs, who also served as the Acting Director of the State Department's policy planning staff during the Bush Administration, highlighted the costs to our foreign policy in a Washington Post article in 2007. Waxman agreed that the benefits of Guantanamo "came at a serious cost." He stated, "…on balance, the prison…has become a drag on America's…global counterterrorism efforts." Specifically, Waxman argued, "the continued controversy over Guantanamo Bay has hampered cooperation with our friends on such critical counterterrorism tasks as information sharing, joint military operations and law enforcement. I know: As a State Department official, I often spent valuable time and diplomatic capital fruitlessly defending our detention practices rather than fostering counterterrorism teamwork. Guantanamo Bay leaves us playing defense and hinders our ability to play effective offense."

Transfer Process

The current process that leads to a transfer decision builds upon the work of the 2009 review task force cited in the overview. It is careful and deliberative. Key features of the transfer process include a comprehensive interagency review and rigorous examination of updated information regarding the detainee, the security situation in the potential host country, and the willingness and capability of the potential host country to implement and ensure compliance with security measures. Those initial reviews are conducted by career professionals, including intelligence analysts, law enforcement agents, and attorneys-- drawn from the Department of Justice, Department of Defense, Department of State, Department of Homeland Security, and Office of the Director of National Intelligence.

Transfer decisions involve an in-depth assessment, often including travel to the potential recipient country by Special Envoys at the Departments of State and Defense, that considers the security situation in the receiving country, and the willingness and capability of the country to comply with security assurances requested by the United States. The Special Envoys negotiate specific security assurances addressing the unique circumstances of each detainee transfer.

Additionally, in making each certification to transfer, the Secretary of Defense consults with the Secretary of State, the Secretary of Homeland Security, the Director of National Intelligence, the Attorney General, and the Chairman of the Joint Chiefs of Staff.

Finally, the Secretary of Defense must clarify that the proposed transfer meets the requirements set forth by Congress in the National Defense Authorization Act. Under Section 1034 of the NDAA for FY 2016, the Secretary may approve the transfer if he certifies that the transfer is in the national security interests of the United States and that actions have been or are planned to be taken that will substantially mitigate the risk of the detainee engaging in terrorist or other hostile activity that threatens the United States or U.S. persons or interests. The factors considered in making this determination include:

- The security situation in the foreign country to which the detainee is to be transferred;
- Confirmed past activities by individuals transferred to the foreign country to which the detainee is to be transferred;

- Actions taken by the United States or the foreign country to reduce the risk the individual will engage in terrorist or hostile activity;

- Security assurances provided by the foreign government

Security Assurances

I cannot discuss the specific security assurances we receive from foreign governments with any degree of specificity in open testimony. However, among the types of security measures that we generally seek are travel restrictions, information sharing, and other measures to satisfy the United States' national security interests and to aid the detainee in reentering society, such as reintegration/rehabilitation programs.

The decision to transfer is made only after detailed, specific conversations with the receiving country about the potential threat a detainee may pose after transfer and the commitment regarding the measures the receiving country will take in order to substantially mitigate that potential threat.

Monitoring of Completed Transfers

Once a detainee is transferred from Guantanamo, the intelligence community and others in the government monitor for indications of reengagement and work closely with liaison partners to ensure the fullest understanding of a former detainee's activities. Through this follow-up process, the United States engages closely our partner nations and may request additional measures. Through a rigorous IC coordination process, that draws on the assessments of eight IC agencies, including the Defense Intelligence Agency and State's Bureau of Intelligence and Research, we determine whether to designate a former detainee as reengaged.

Reengagement

A primary concern regarding a potential transfer is whether a detainee will "return to the fight" or otherwise reengage in acts that threaten the United States or U.S. persons or interests. We take the possibility of reengagement very seriously. Secretary Carter has emphasized that safety is his first priority when considering a transfer.

The most recent public data on reengagement of former Guantanamo detainees was released earlier this month and is current as of January 15, 2016.

The Office of the Director of National Intelligence (ODNI) categorizes the figures in three ways: 1) Total, 2) Pre-22 January 2009, which refers to former detainees who departed Guantanamo prior to 22 January 2009, and 3) Post-22 January 2009, which refers to former detainees who departed Guantanamo after January 22, 2009.

- **Total: 17.5%** confirmed of reengaging (118 of 676); **12.7%** suspected of reengaging (86 of 676)

- **Pre-22 January 2009: 20.9%** confirmed of reengaging (111 of 532); **13.9%** suspected of reengaging (74 of 532)

- **Post-22 January 2009: 4.9%** confirmed of reengaging (7 of 144); **8.3%** suspected of reengaging (12of 144)

In other words, the rate of reengagement has been much lower for those transferred since 2009.

According to publicly available information released by ODNI, over 85% of detainees transferred since 2009 are neither confirmed nor suspected of having reengaged. This statistic speaks to the result of the careful scrutiny given to each transfer by the intensive interagency review process, and the negotiation of security assurances sufficient to prevent detainees from posing a continuing threat to the United States and its allies and partners after they have been transferred.

We take any indications of suspected or confirmed reengagement very seriously, and we work in close coordination with our partners to mitigate reengagement and to take follow-on action when necessary. This is demonstrated by an additional point about the reengagement data: of the 118 former Guantanamo detainees confirmed of reengaging (the vast majority of whom were transferred prior to 2009), 55 are now either dead or in foreign custody.

Plan to Close Guantanamo Detention Facility

I will now turn to the Administration's Plan for Guantanamo Detention Closure, which was submitted to Congress on February 23, 2016. This plan represents the collective best judgment of the Administration's top military and civilian leaders.

I want to note the outstanding job that DOD personnel from the offices of Detainee Policy, Comptroller and Acquisition and Technology and Logistics who did in helping to put together this plan.

As President Obama stated in announcing the plan, it has four main elements.

First, we will continue the process of responsibly transferring the 36 detainees currently eligible for transfer.

Second, we will accelerate the PRB process to ensure that each detainee receives an initial review.

Third, we will continue to look for individual dispositions for detainees, including the prosecution of detainees in the military commissions process, and if possible, in the federal courts or in foreign courts. Currently, 7 detainees are being actively prosecuted under the military commission process, 5 are accused of the 9/11 attacks, 1 is charged with the bombing of the *USS Cole*, and 1 is charged with actions as a senior al Qaeda commander. In addition, **3** are in the sentencing phase or are serving sentences pursuant to their convictions.

Fourth, we are working with the Congress to identify a secure domestic detention location for the limited number of detainees who remain designated for continued detention and who are not candidates for U.S. prosecution or detention or transfer to a foreign country

The Department of Defense looked at past reviews and surveyed potential detention locations in the United States. The Department determined that there exist facilities in the United States that could safely, securely, and humanely house Guantanamo detainees.

Key factors included time needed for modifications, disruption to existing missions (moving current prisoners), distance to medical facilities and transportation sites, troop support and housing, and force-protection and security requirements. The Department concluded that a single detention center was the most efficient plan for continued military commissions and continued law of war detention.

Transfer to the United States of a small number of Guantanamo detainees will require modifications to meet standards for secure and humane treatment of detainees under international law.

The plan focuses on working with the Congress to identify a domestic location for the small number of detainees who remain designated for continued detention and who are not candidates for U.S. prosecution or detention or transfer to a foreign country. Under the Administration's closure plan, these detainees would be relocated to a secure detention facility in the United States.

The taxpayers are paying too high a financial price to keep the Guantanamo Bay detention facility open. As Representative Adam Smith, the Ranking Member of the House Armed Services Committee regularly comments, "it is wildly expensive." The plan submitted to the Congress last month highlights this issue. The Department of Defense estimates that recurring costs at Guantanamo would be between $65 million and $85 million higher annually than at a detention facility located in the United States. Transition costs to a domestic detention facility would be offset within three to five years due to the lower operating costs of a U.S. facility. Moving Guantanamo detainees to the United States could generate at least $335 million in net savings over 10 years and up to $1/7billion in net savings over 20 years.

Many of the former retired flag and general officers who wrote to the Senate Armed Services Committee last year, also wrote a letter to the leaders of that Committee and to the House Armed Services Committee on March 1 of this year, urging consideration of the Administration's closure plan as a foundation to "find a path to finally shutter the detention facility."

The Department of Justice, in consultation with the Secretary of Defense, submitted a report to Congress in 2015 that concluded that if detainees were relocated to the United States, existing statutory safeguards and executive and congressional authorities provide robust protection of national security. The current transfer provisions, however, restrict the Government's ability to prosecute detainees in the United States, even if it represents the best – or only – option for bringing a detainee to justice. The President has consistently opposed these restrictions, which curtail options for reducing the detainee population. We look forward to working with Congress on lifting these restrictions. Submission of the Administration's plan continues this process of cooperation.

Legal Authorities and Legislative Relief

To carry out the plan to close the detention facility at Guantanamo, the Administration will work with Congress to modify the transfer restrictions in sections 1031 and 1032 of the National Defense Authorization Act of 2016.

Moreover, in its Report Pursuant to Section 1039 of the National Defense Authorization Act for Fiscal Year 2014, the Department of Justice addressed the issues of whether a Guantanamo detainee relocated to the United States could be eligible for certain forms of relief from removal, or release from immigration detention, or could have related constitutional rights. The Department of Justice concluded that existing statutory safeguards and executive and congressional authorities provide robust protection of national security. The report stated that historically, the courts have treated detainees held under the laws of war who are brought to the United States as outside the reach of the immigration laws; and that Congress separately has authority to provide by statute that the immigration laws generally, as well as particular forms of relief, are inapplicable to any Guantanamo detainees held in the United States pursuant to the 2001 Authorization for the Use of Military Force.

Conclusion

Finally, I would like to take a moment to recognize the military service members conducting detention operations at Guantanamo Bay. Too often in the course of considering the future of the detention facility, we lose sight of the remarkable men and women who serve honorably under extraordinarily difficult conditions. They have our deepest appreciation for their service and the professionalism they display each and every day on behalf of our Nation.

President Bush worked towards closing Guantanamo, and many officials in his Administration worked hard towards that objective. We are closer to this goal than many people may realize. Of the nearly 800 detainees to have been held at Guantanamo since the facility opened in 2002, the vast majority have already been transferred, including more than 500 detainees transferred by the previous Administration. The President and the national security experts of this Administration believe it should be closed. The senior military leaders of the country and the leaders of the Department of Defense concur. As indicated in the letter by the retired military leaders, many believe closure of this facility is the single most important counterterrorism effort the United States can undertake. We believe the issue is not whether to close the Guantanamo Bay detention facility; the issue is how to do it.

Thank you, and I look forward to your questions.

Chairman ROYCE. Let me ask both our witnesses. The Secretary of Defense and Attorney General Lynch have both stated that transfers of Guantanamo detainees to the United States are legally prohibited. Is that your understanding of the law as well?

Mr. WOLOSKY. It's my understanding of the law that with the statute in its current form prohibits transfers to the United States, which is why we are working at this time with the Congress or seeking to work with the Congress to modify the law in order to be able to bring into the United States a small, reducible minimum number of detainees as described in the President's closure plan.

Chairman ROYCE. Is it correct then that under current law the Department of Defense is prohibited from selecting any U.S. site or making any preparations for transfer of the detainees to the U.S.

Mr. WOLOSKY. Frankly, I have no idea. That is a legal question that is most appropriately directed to the Department of Defense.

Chairman ROYCE. Mr. Lewis?

Mr. LEWIS. Mr. Chairman, we believe detainees can be safely and securely and humanely detained in the United States. I believe the current statute does prohibit us from doing that.

So we are working toward doing that. The plan that was sent up we gave a look at locations, military facilities and Federal and state facilities that could do that. We believe detainees, as I said, can be detained. We did not pick a specific location.

Chairman ROYCE. One of the concerns that Congress clearly has here is that in terms of our experience with those who have left Guantanamo Bay, over the long haul those that returned to the fight or those who are suspected of having returned to the fight is a little over 30 percent.

I understand the argument that the administration is making that of recent individuals released, they haven't returned—there's a lower percentage that return to the fight.

But, of course, there's a continuum in terms of collecting the information and monitoring and transitioning as people end up—I'm just looking at the overall number. The overall number is in the neighborhood of 31 percent, and if we begin to focus on some of the recent examples of those who did, it is pretty concerning, given Ibrahim al-Qosi. He was one of the high-risk detainees, transferred by this administration and by 2014 he had joined al-Qaeda in the Arabian Peninsula and now he is in their leadership.

And last month we saw a video urging a takeover in Saudi Arabia. He would not be out doing his propaganda if he were housed in Guantanamo and one of the concerns I have about the rap sheet on those inside as we make the argument—we've been through these discussions—when we make the argument about the necessity of releasing them.

But the fact is—but the bottom line is they end up, a certain percentage of them, pulling stunts like this, calling for the overthrow of the Government of Saudi Arabia and very engaged in that process.

And so in terms of the—I understand the theory that it's a recruitment tool—that thesis. But the fact is that a significant percentage of them return to the fight and we have an unclassified letter to Congress last month from the director of national intelligence writing that the intelligence community lacks reporting that Guantanamo propaganda has motivated more recent ISIS recruits to join the group.

So there is a debate. I certainly talked to former administration high ranking officers and officials who have the opposite of the view that you've laid out today who tell me no, they don't think it has to do with recruitment.

We understand your theory on it. But there is the fact, and the fact is that we do have this process. So let me ask you this question.

We do have this challenge because of the way this process is releasing individuals to countries that don't have the capabilities. So here's my question.

Mr. Lewis lists in his testimony some of the countries that the administration has transferred detainees to since 2009. So Mr. Lewis, El Salvador, Kazakhstan, Ghana, and I would just ask Lee, have you been to Ghana?

Now, this is one of the countries that I've been to. Are you fully confident that it has the capability and motivation to monitor and track these detainees?

Mr. WOLOSKY. Mr. Chairman, yes, we are. As you know, no transfer occurs unless we are confident in the security assurances that we've received and the Secretary of Defense makes the requisite certifications to the Congress.

To date, and we only have admittedly several months of experience, what I can tell you in this open forum—and we're happy to come and brief you in closed session—is that we are very pleased by the implementation by the Government of Ghana of the security assurances that have been agreed to.

Chairman ROYCE. As I said, I've been to Ghana and across West Africa. Ghana is a wonderful place. It's a wonderful country. But the fact is that it doesn't have top notch intelligence or law enforcement services to deal with this kind of problem.

The GDP per capita is, like, $4,000. It's 175th in the world. The fact is that their leaders have many, many challenges in Ghana facing them every day. So I'm going to guess that tracking and monitoring former Guantanamo detainees isn't a priority just as it wasn't in other examples that I've laid for you—laid out for you like Uruguay.

It just wasn't high up there and if they weren't returning or if 31 percent of them haven't returned to the fight this wouldn't be a concern. But this is a very real concern.

I'll go to Mr. Engel for his questioning.

Mr. ENGEL. Thank you, Mr. Chairman.

You know, emotionally—because of terrorists and the attacks on 9/11 and the attacks in Brussels and things that we're hearing—emotionally, you just want to say well, throw them all in jail and put them all in jail and throw away the key.

But that's not how were supposed to work as a nation. That's not what we stand for, and I don't believe that we should abandon our principles if we can still be safe.

I would say that things are a trade-off. I wouldn't be for abandoning our principles if it meant that there was going to be a larger chance of being unsafe as a result of releasing or transferring some of these people.

But when you read the facts and you look at the facts, you see that it's really worse by keeping them there. I have a balance sheet.

I'm not for releasing anybody who was guilty, but I'm also not for keeping people in prison year after year after year with no trial. That's not what I learned when I was in grade school about one of the reasons why this country is so great.

Opponents of closing the Guantanamo detention facility often say that the people currently in the prison are the worst of the worst or the most dangerous, and that's why we should not release them at all.

Some critics point to risk assessments from the previous administration—from the Bush administration—in support of this claim.

What's your view of how risk assessments have been conducted by the interagency task force and the periodic review boards compared with previous risk assessments.

And given what you know about detainees currently held at Guantanamo, are they really the most dangerous? If not, why have they been in Guantanamo for so long?

Is it because we've already transferred all the easy cases? Explain how these people are vis-a-vis cases that have already been adjudicated.

Mr. WOLOSKY. Sure. Thank you, Congressman, for the question.

It's certainly the case that there are some extremely dangerous individuals who remain in Guantanamo.

But it's also the case that there are individuals in the Guantanamo who are not extremely dangerous. Of the 36 that are currently approved for transfer, 29 are Yemeni nationals and, of course, we have been unable to return them to Yemen. Returning them to the country of origin is always our first choice in removing a Guantanamo detainee from Guantanamo.

So there is a significant component of country of origin that goes into the remaining detainee population and while they are still there.

With respect to your first question, it sort of bleeds into the re-engagement issues that the chairman raised which I appreciate the opportunity to address because we actually do have hard data on re-engagement and I'd like to refer you to the numbers in the report issued by the Office of Director of National Intelligence earlier this month on re-engagement.

The actual numbers are, in this administration, seven confirmed re-engagement former detainees. In the previous administration, 111.

Seven in this administration out of 144 transferred. That translates into 4.9 percent. The number for the previous administration is 111 out of 532, which translates into 20.9 percent.

We believe that this data affirms that the procedures that we have put in place during this administration have worked to substantially reduce any re-engagement concerns.

And I also think that you're exactly right when you indicated in your opening statement that the risks of transferring detainees, and we've acknowledged that there are risks, must be weighed against the risks of keeping the facility open.

There has been until recently a bipartisan consensus that there are significant national security and foreign policy risks associated with keeping the facility open.

That was articulated by the previous President who transferred over 500 detainees out of Guantanamo in furtherance of his effort to close Guantanamo because he recognized that it was a propaganda tool.

The conclusion was also reached by nonpartisan military leaders across the services. So I think that when we talk—I'll stop speaking in a moment—when we talk about re-engagement it is important to refer to the actual data that has been put forward by the director of national intelligence.

Mr. ENGEL. Let me ask you, who's left at Guantanamo? Is it correct that of the 91 individuals who remain at Guantanamo, 81 are not facing criminal charges? Is that true, and is it also correct that 35 individuals have been cleared for transfer out of Guantanamo?

So what does that mean to be transferred out? Who decides? How long have they been cleared for transfer and why are they still waiting to leave?

Mr. WOLOSKY. Thank you for your question.

There are 91 detainees in Guantanamo. Thirty-six have been approved for transfer. Some of them have been approved for transfer since 2010, some of them more recently.

Ten are in some stage of the military commission process either facing charges or serving sentences and the remainder, 40 some odd detainees, are neither approved for transfer nor currently facing charges.

Mr. ENGEL. Can I—Mr. Chairman, could you just indulge me?

I just want to quickly ask a Federal court question. The administration's plan calls for some Guantanamo detainees to be tried in the U.S. Federal courts, but Congress has imposed a ban on transferring any Guantanamo detainees to the U.S. for any reason including for trial.

But from what I can see, Federal courts have been extremely effective at trying terrorism cases. Since 9/11, Federal courts have convicted over 500 people on terrorism-related offenses. By contrast, the 9/11 military commission trial has been in pre-trial hearings since 2012.

So the trial itself is not expected to start until 2020. So, why have the Federal courts, in your opinion, been so much more effective at bringing these terrorists to justice?

Mr. WOLOSKY. Well, the Federal courts have a proven mechanism for both convicting and then making sure that convicted felons serve time safely and responsibly.

You're right, there are numerous terrorists who have been effectively convicted and are now serving time in the Federal prison system. Faisal Shahzad, the Times Square bomber, Richard Reid, the shoe bomber, Mr. Tsarnaev, the Boston Marathon bomber, Moussaoui—the list goes on. They all have been held safely and securely.

Back to the point that the chairman raised about Mr. Al-Qosi. I should point out that he was released from the custody of the United States after serving his military commission sentence.

So he is an example of someone who went through the military commission system, pled guilty to materiel support and conspiracy and then after he served his sentence in that system he was released.

If he were put through the Article 3 system, he would probably still be serving his sentence and not be off doing what he's been doing.

Chairman ROYCE. If I could—we're talking about two different sets of numbers. So if I could just address that quickly before we go to the next member.

In terms of the administration's numbers that they released, the administration's claim is 7.9 percent of detainees released under the President are confirmed or suspected of reengaging in terrorism.

You were just using the number of confirmed and the administration that released a figure that overall the rate is just over 31 percent. Investigators tell us that it takes 4 years to confirm.

So there is—there is a question in terms of the time line on detainees' recidivism. But the overall rate that I'm quoting here is the rate on confirmed or suspected.

We'll go now to Mr. Chris Smith of New Jersey.

Mr. SMITH. Thank you very much, Mr. Chairman, and welcome, both of you, to the committee.

Yesterday, I chaired an oversight hearing focusing on the 14 countries that Reuters found after a series of investigative reports. I want this on the record and I hope the press will take notice of this because I think it's an egregious flaw in our implementation of the Trafficking Victims Protection Act, which I am the author of.

I am deeply concerned that Cuba's tier, their State Department ranking, which had been the worst—it had been there during the Bush administration, had been so designated during the Obama administration—only to be manipulated politically for non-human trafficking criteria in anticipation of this rapprochement, which I find absurd.

The TIP Report should be absolutely accurate and speak truth to power and defend those who have been—are you bored with this?

Mr. WOLOSKY. No. No.

Mr. SMITH. Thank you. Should speak truth to power when it comes to sex trafficking and child sex tourism, which is rampant, and the Castro regime gleans enormous profits from it as they do from labor trafficking.

And we have an upgrade which takes them off the sanctions list, which I find to be appalling. Yesterday one of our witnesses pointed out that the Cuban Government is likely one of the largest and most profitable trafficking promoters in the entire world.

So my hope is that this year, and yesterday's title of our hearing was next time get it right, that there will be no political manipulation of the trafficking tiers.

If you read the report itself, it reads inescapably to a tier three sanctions rating. But when it got to another level there was a manipulation there for political reasons and I find that appalling and deeply, deeply saddening.

Let me just ask you a question on point. The point man in Uruguay, as we all know, for overseeing the six transferred Guantanamo detainees is the Minister of Interior, Eduardo Bonomi.

Are you confident in Minister Bonomi's commitment to ensuring that the former detainees do not link up with international Islamic terrorist networks or ensuring that these six individuals do not threaten our Embassy personnel or American nationals in Uruguay?

In other words, do you trust Eduardo Bonomi and believe he is a man of honorable character?

Mr. WOLOSKY. Well, thank you for your question, Congressman.

I don't know him but what I can say is that we are confident. There's never—as I said, there's never no risk associated with transferring a detainee. The appropriate calculus, we believe, is the one essentially that Congressman Engel put forth, which is weighing the risks of transferring versus the risks which have been recognized across the spectrum of maintaining the facility.

But we are confident, to your question, that the Government of Uruguay is taking appropriate steps to substantially mitigate the risk associate with each of the six detainees that have been transferred to its custody.

Mr. SMITH. Again, is it your view that the minister—this particular minister, an avowed leftist, is trustworthy? Because he is the guardian.

Mr. WOLOSKY. I don't agree with that necessarily. When we look at countries to resettle detainees in we do not base it on personalities.

We base it on the government as a whole, the capabilities of the government as a whole and the willingness of the government, and then of course the specific security assurances that have been negotiated and our assessment of whether or not can and will be implemented.

Mr. SMITH. Well, since he is likely to be the point man or is the point man, could you provide for the record at least your analysis as to his trustworthiness?

Mr. WOLOSKY. I can't because I don't know him. But, again, when we look at transfer opportunities we base our conclusions on the capabilities of the government.

Mr. SMITH. But he is the point person for the government.

Mr. WOLOSKY. He may be now. He may not be tomorrow and so we don't—we don't rely on particular personalities is sort of the bottom line.

Mr. SMITH. I understand. But with all due respect, personnel is policy and if a government has a person walking point on a particular issue like this one and it happens to be this Minister of Interior, I think we would want to know whether or not he is a person who can be trusted, particularly with such people who have committed terrorism and may recommit.

Mr. WOLOSKY. Well, again, as I said, I have not met him so I feel uncomfortable offering a personal assessment and what we do do is we base our decisions on governments as a whole.

Mr. SMITH. But, again, that's why—for the record if you could provide an additional amplification of those who analysed the situation and felt comfortable enough to proceed with this vis-a-vis this particular minister.

Mr. WOLOSKY. The Department of State felt comfortable.

Mr. SMITH. If you could provide us that analysis in a follow-up—just answer.

Mr. WOLOSKY. Just to be clear, what—the analysis of——

Chairman ROYCE. And we can do a lot of that by follow-up and answer because we need to go to Mr. David Cicilline and get through a lot of members here.

Mr. Cicilline, you're next.

Mr. CICILLINE. Thank you, Mr. Chairman, and thank you to our witnesses.

The title of this hearing refers to the foreign policy and national security costs of the administration's plan to close Guantanamo Bay, the detention facility.

However, the vast majority of national security leaders, as you both indicated, as well as leaders on both sides of the political spectrum, say that the real foreign policy and national security costs come as a result of keeping the prison open and in fact describe the closing of the Guantanamo detention facility is a national security imperative.

And so I'd like you to speak to how the administration's plan to close Guantanamo Bay detention facility will impact our ability to work with our coalition partners in the fight against terror and how the failure to close it is providing a real impediment to that critical work.

Mr. LEWIS. Thank you, sir.

As I noted in my opening statement, continuously countries across the world and allies tell us that Gitmo hurts us. So we work with those countries.

By closing Gitmo we address a concern of the rest of the world. The United States needs to lead. We can't do this alone, and when our allies in counterterrorism are telling us that Gitmo needs to be closed we take an issue off the table.

We don't remove the risk completely. It's always going to be a propaganda issue but we take that issue off the table.

Mr. CICILLINE. And does the presence of Guantanamo Bay have an impact on our ability to use diplomacy and soft power to press other countries to uphold human rights obligations including responsibilities against torture, forced disappearance, arbitrary or definite detention—things that we speak about with other countries—and has our credibility been harmed by the continued indefinite detentions at Guantanamo Bay and the opening of this facility?

Mr. LEWIS. Yes, sir, I believe it does. As the President noted in his statement last month, leaders that he meets with continuously raise the issue of Gitmo. They continuously raise the issue of specific detainees.

Lee's predecessor, Cliff Sloan, mentioned how he's been told by foreign leaders that closing Gitmo would be the single greatest issue to help our counterterrorism efforts and repeated leaders from both this administration and the previous administration have said the same. So I think it does hurt us.

Mr. CICILLINE. And with respect to the 36 detainees that have been approved for transfer, some since 2010, what is the—what is taking so long for that to be completed?

Mr. LEWIS. As we said, most of them are Yemenis. Twenty-nine are Yemenis so we can't confidently send them to Yemen right now.

So we have to go look at this list of 27 other countries that have stepped up and find a fit for that detainee, find a fit for the security situation in the country, their willingness, and their capacity.

So it's a mixture of sequencing. It's a mixture of the domestic issues in the country. But 27 countries demonstrates that there are countries that want to help us and are willing to step up.

We are confident that the majority of these 36 can be transferred the next several months.

Mr. CICILLINE. Thank you. And with respect to the issues regarding reengagement, the office of the director of national intelligence categorizes these reengagement in three different ways for these purposes of this hearing.

Seventeen and a half percent of detainees have pre-engaged. But if you break that number down prior to this President, prior to January 2009, the number was 20.9 percent. But since President Obama the figure if 4.9 percent.

So Mr. Wolosky, will you explain are those figures accurate? What do they represent and how do you account for this dramatic reduction in reengagement, which is critical? I mean, those are—obviously, any reengagement is alarming but the fact that it's been brought to 4.9 percent from 20 percent didn't happen just by magic. There has to have been some change in process. Could you speak to that?

Mr. WOLOSKY. Sure. Yes, there have been many changes in process that have been put in place in this administration from the actual decision to approve someone for transfer, which is a complicated, time-consuming and very thorough and very rigorous interagency process and only moves forward with the consent of each of six agency and departments.

Two, then the actual decision to transfer and approve for transfer detainee to a specific country which, again, is a rigorous interagency process that entails the negotiation of detailed and quite specific security assurances with the specific country and then ultimately input from the same six agencies and departments and then congressional notification by the Secretary of Defense.

So our process is very thorough and it's very rigorous and it's very time-consuming, further to your question about why things have taken so long and we believe that, again, there's never no risk.

But we believe that the relative success of our processes are reflected in the reengagement figures when you look at the figure—the small figure in this administration and the larger figure in the previous administration.

Mr. CICILLINE. Thank you, and I yield back. Thank you, Mr. Chairman.

Chairman ROYCE. Mr. Rohrabacher.

Mr. ROHRABACHER. Well, the first question I'd like answered I think could be answered with a yes or no.

Has the Defense Department ever knowingly transferred a detainee to a country that did not exhibit an ability to substantially mitigate the risk or maintain control of that individual? I think a yes or no could be—it's a very straightforward.

Has the Defense Department ever sent someone to a country knowing that that country was unable to keep control of that person?

Mr. LEWIS. No.

Mr. WOLOSKY. Well, I'm not from Defense Department but I'm assuming that your question relates to this administration while that was the statutory standard.

Mr. ROHRABACHER. Actually, it doesn't. Do you know of any examples?

Mr. WOLOSKY. I can't speak for the previous administration, certainly.

Mr. ROHRABACHER. Okay. Well, what about this administration? Can you speak to whether or not that the Defense Department has transferred a detainee to someone who—is there some reason that you can't say yes or no?

Mr. LEWIS. I don't work at the Department of Defense so——

Mr. ROHRABACHER. All right. But you——

Mr. LEWIS. So what I can tell you is——

Mr. ROHRABACHER. Let's leave it at knowingly. Do you know of a case where the Defense Department has knowingly transferred a detainee to a country that did not exhibit the ability to substantially mitigate the risk by maintaining control of the individual? Do you know of a case like that?

Mr. WOLOSKY. I do not.

Mr. ROHRABACHER. Okay.

Mr. LEWIS. So the statutory standard is——

Mr. ROHRABACHER. It's all right. It's all right.

Mr. LEWIS. Yes, sir.

Mr. ROHRABACHER. You made your answer.

Let me just suggest that this idea that people throughout the world are so upset with us for keeping a significant number of people who were captured as part of terrorist units—incarcerating them in Guantanamo, that that is such a horror story that it's a recruitment vehicle—that's what the President is telling us. It's what the administration is telling us.

Let me suggest if that is true than our European allies and some others believe that taking these hardened murderers who murder men, women, and children and incarcerating them in Cuba or anywhere else—let me suggest that that attitude of Europe may well be changing in the next 6 months or so when they realize that the slaughter that's taking place in Paris and now in Brussels is part of an international movement to destroy Western civilization and replace it with a caliphate.

And when they understand that, my guess is that view that it's so bad to keep these people in prison will change as well.

Let me ask you this. We say that about 30 percent or whatever that figure is that have been released have returned to terrorist activities.

How many lives have been lost by those terrorists who went back to their terrorist activity? How many lives?

Mr. LEWIS. I can talk about that in a classified setting but——

Mr. ROHRABACHER. Oh, classified?

Mr. LEWIS. Yes.

Mr. ROHRABACHER. Oh, it's going to—so is it over ten?

Mr. LEWIS. So what I can tell you is, unfortunately, there have been Americans that have died because of Gitmo detainees.

Mr. ROHRABACHER. How many Americans have to die? How many people in Brussels or Paris have to die, civilians? What's the threshold at that point—well, maybe we will keep them under control in Gitmo?

Mr. LEWIS. When anybody dies it's a tragedy and we don't want anybody to die because we transferred detainees.

However, it's the best judgment and the considered judgment of this administration and the previous administration that the risk of keeping Gitmo open is outweighed—that we should close Gitmo, that the risk——

Mr. ROHRABACHER. So the innocent people who are going to lose their lives because of this they're just part of the equation?

Mr. LEWIS. No, sir. There are risks——

Mr. ROHRABACHER. I'm sorry. I want to tell you this much. As far as I'm concerned if one child is saved because she would have been blown up by someone who's being released it's better to keep all 90 of those people in Gitmo, and this idea that the people of the world oh, they're so upset with us that it's a recruiting vehicle, that we've kept terrorists who murder innocent people in Gitmo, well, you know what? I think the bigger recruiting tool today is when our Government, especially this administration, is perceived as being weak.

I think terrorists are recruited not because we've held other terrorists in prison but because we look like we're weak and cannot deal with the challenge.

This disgusts me. Thank you very much.

Chairman ROYCE. We go to Robin Kelly of Illinois.

Ms. KELLY. Thank you, Mr. Chair.

Mr. Wolosky, yesterday I returned from Cuba with President Obama's delegation where we discussed the opening of U.S.-Cuban relations.

While we have made steps toward developing positive bilateral relations, President Castro has repeatedly stated that relations with the United States will never be fully normal so long as the United States occupies or utilizes the Guantanamo Bay detention facility.

How do you imagine the continued use of the Guantanamo Bay detention facility would affect the process of normalizing relations between the United States and Cuba?

Mr. WOLOSKY. Thank you, ma'am.

As the President has said, this administration has no plans to turn over the base at Guantanamo Bay, Cuba. We are intent, as you know, to close the detention facility at that base.

We would expect to continue to use the base for dealing with mass migration contingencies and also to support Coast Guard operations with respect to counter drug operations in the region.

Ms. KELLY. Okay. To what extent do you believe this local diplomatic security could contribute to advancing our national security efforts?

Mr. WOLOSKY. Well, as you know, President Obama feels firmly that closing Guantanamo is in the national security interests of the United States.

No detainee is transferred from Guantanamo absent a certification from the Secretary of Defense that the transfer will—the specific transfer will further the national security of the United States.

And as I said in my opening statement, President Obama was hardly the first U.S. President to conclude that closing Guantanamo was in the national security and foreign policy interests of the United States.

The first President to do that was the man who opened it up, George W. Bush, who concluded that it was a propaganda tool and a distraction to our allies. Not only did he believe that, he acted on it in transferring over 500 detainees from Guantanamo to third countries.

So we believe, as did President Bush, as did numerous former Secretaries of State of both parties, the same for Secretaries of Defense, same for three former Chairmen of the Joint Chiefs of Staff and numerous retired flag officers, that closing Guantanamo will on balance enhance our national security.

As we have said, you cannot live life without risk and the proper analysis, as Congressman Engel suggested, we believe is balancing the risks of keeping it open versus the risks of closing it and, you know, we work diligently to prevent reengagement.

We've been quite successful in this administration in preventing reengagement and even one detainee returning to the fight is too many. But the proper analysis is balancing the risks of closure versus the risks of keeping it open.

And I would point out that, obviously, our hearts go out to the people of Belgium today and our hearts went out to the people of Paris just a few short months ago.

But the continued maintenance of the facility at Guantanamo Bay did not prevent either of those attacks.

There are, unfortunately, going to be acts of terrorism, probably whether the facility is opened or closed. The proper analysis is what are the risks of keeping it open in light of the very obvious use of the that facility as a propaganda tool which, frankly, you should not have to question.

ISIL, which has now claimed responsibility for the Belgium attacks, uses Guantanamo as a propaganda tool. There's no question about this.

We've all seen images of prisoners taken by ISIL being executed wearing orange jumpsuits that we believe are meant to mimic and invoke Guantanamo jumpsuits.

There's no question that this is being used as a propaganda tool as President Bush himself concluded when he determined to close the facility.

Ms. KELLY. I'm running out of time. So thank you. I yield back.

Chairman ROYCE. Matt Salmon of Arizona.

Mr. SALMON. Thank you, Mr. Chairman.

As long as we're talking about Cuba policy, I've got something I'd like to get off my chest.

I find the imagery of the President yukking it up with FARC terrorists at a baseball game yesterday when Europe is under siege by terrorists disgusting, absolutely disgusting, and I believe that, well, I'm not going to go on on that. I just think there are better things I think the public should be seeing.

One of the troubling aspects of the transfer of the six detainees to Uruguay was the Sloan letter, the letter assuring the Uruguayan Government that none of the detainees had ever been associated with terrorism. We know this isn't true, and I know it was your predecessor who wrote the letter. Can you walk us through how the administration could make such a misleading statement?

How can you expect a host government to then take seriously the monitoring and mitigation of the detainee? In Uruguay's case, the government stated ahead of time they would not monitor the detainees and we still released them.

Does this speak to the administration's overall willingness to accept greater risk in pursuit of the President's political goal to empty the prison? Mr. Wolosky.

Mr. WOLOSKY. Sure. Yes, sir. Thank you.

First, although we cannot speak in an open session about the specifics of the security assurances that have been agreed to with any one country, I can assure you that any public statements you may have just referenced are not accurate and we do have security assurances with Uruguay.

We briefed this committee in closed session on those security assurances. We're happy to come and brief you about what they are and how they're being implemented.

As to the Sloan letter, what I can tell you is that the conclusions in the Sloan letter mirrored the conclusions reached by the executive—the EOTF process, which was the process put in place at the beginning of this administration to carefully review all reasonably available information to the U.S. Government with respect to a particular detainee.

That process was described in some detail in my written submission. It involved dozens of national security professionals from all relevant agencies and departments of the government including the intelligence community, many of them career professionals, and they reached certain conclusions about each detainee and the information available to the United States about each detainee.

So what the Cliff Sloan letter does is it attracts the conclusion of the EOTF report, which was this comprehensive interagency review that was conducted for the specific purpose of analyzing the available information in the U.S. Government about each detainee and then making a disposition recommendation about that detainee.

Mr. SALMON. Whatever justification you're trying to make for why the letter, though inaccurate, was sent doesn't really provide a lot of comfort to most of us.

The fact is it was flat out wrong. It was an error and a gross error. In a recent interview with NPR you said that after having visited Guantanamo Bay you felt the detention center was better certainly than any state or local correctional facility or prison you visited and better than many of the Federal facilities. Yet, you're advising the President on the closure of this facility so we can propose building a new facility here. Does that make any sense?

Would it not be better to tell the American people and the world the real story about the facility, that it's a model detention facility, that the International Committee of the Red Cross, the ICRC, has regular access to it?

Wouldn't it be best to dispel the false narrative that some use, rather than close down what by your estimation is a great facility?

Mr. WOLOSKY. Well, I do think it's a professionally run and a humanely run facility and in particular the servicemen and women who serve there face enormous hardship in their service and they do an outstanding job in running the facility.

General Kelly did an outstanding job in managing that. Now Admiral Tidd has taken over that process, and they both do an incredible job in maintaining what is a very well-run facility.

That said, we still think it should be closed.

Chairman ROYCE. We're going to Greg Meeks of New York and then Mo Brooks of Alabama.

Mr. MEEKS. Thank you, Mr. Chairman.

I just want to get, first, a couple of things straight, you know, for the record.

As I listened and my heart goes out to those individuals who lost their lives recently in Belgium as well as, you know, we talk about the Paris attacks often and you talk about—I just want to make sure that everyone and the record is clear that this war is not just against the West.

We don't talk about all of the attacks that have taken place in various places. It's taken place—and we should be just as concerned in Nigeria, in Kenya, in Turkey.

So to think—these are all human lives. We ought to be concerned about all of those lives, not just in one area. And it's not just against us.

It's not just against Christians because when you look at that Muslims have been killed also by these thugs and that should be properly noted. And it should also be clear, and I think that the historical record is clear, that when we act out of fear our nation has made monumental mistakes, and keeping Gitmo in operation out of fear—because that's what I'm hearing.

Folks are saying out of fear we need to keep Gitmo—we beget another monumental mistake that, one, hurts America's interest rather than helps it.

You know, what comes straight to mind is we acted out of fear when we put the Japanese into internment camps. And so therefore I caution us. And then after it happens then we say oh, look at our past or we try to not talk about what we did.

And so history gives us a reminder of what we should or should not be doing in this place and calmer heads and better heads as opposed to acting out of fear and emotion.

So I just think that the record should be clear on that and it should be clear that all kinds of lives are lost in all parts of the world.

And so this is a threat to everybody—not just to the West, not just to Christians but to everybody and that's why we've got to band together and work together in a cooperative manner.

That being said, let me ask a quick question. Where do we go? If the Guantanamo detention facilities close—we close them—what will the United States do when we capture terrorist suspects in the future?

Do we have other adequate facilities for these individuals and how would the administration in the future capture, detention, and interrogation of high-level ISIS commanders?

Mr. LEWIS. Thank you, sir.

We do believe we have the facilities. We do—any future captures would be considered on a case by case basis and we'd consider whether the host nation could detain them or whether there'd be a disposition under prosecution, either Article 3, possibly military commissions.

But we believe we have the abilities. We've shown one or two cases in Iraq recently to detain people and then turn them over to the host country. But it's on a case by case basis.

Mr. MEEKS. So there is a clear and concrete plan on how we would do this?

Mr. LEWIS. Yes, sir.

Mr. MEEKS. Now, let me ask also. I was listening to some of the debate earlier and there was a question about recidivism rates and I guess according to the official reports from the office of the director of national intelligence that fewer than 5 percent of detainees that are transferred by the Obama administration are confirmed to have engaged in terrorist attacks.

But I did hear—I think it was Chairman Royce—talk about they used a reengagement rate that is 30 percent. Now, is it 30? Can you describe how you make that determination—how those rates are determined and why was there such a disparity?

Mr. WOLOSKY. Well, I'll let the chairman speak for himself. But I think that——

Chairman ROYCE. Will the gentleman yield? I will speak. Because it's confirmed and suspected and you're leaving out suspected.

Mr. WOLOSKY. Not in this administration, respectfully, sir. The rate of suspected in this administration is 8.3 percent.

Chairman ROYCE. No, that's the exact numbers that I concur are right and the overall numbers are over 30 percent overall.

And 8.9 confirmed and suspected, and as explained to us the investigators say it takes about 4 years lead time in order to get all of the confirmation. I've just explained—I yield back.

Mr. WOLOSKY. There were over 530 detainees transferred during the previous administration. Obviously, we cannot speak to the circumstances under with those detainees were transferred.

First, how was the decision made to transfer them. Second, how was the decision made to transfer them to a specific country. Third, what assurances, if any, did the previous administration obtain from the third country to keep us and them safe.

We can't speak to that. All we can do is speak to what we are doing in this administration.

Mr. MEEKS. And that's what I want you to do, speak to——

Mr. WOLOSKY. What we are doing in this administration is at both stages of the process, first, making a determination in principle that a detainee may be approved for transfer and designated as such and, second, transferring him to a specific country subject to specific and detailed security assurances.

What we are doing is very thorough. It's interagency. It's very comprehensive and it takes a long time. It's described at length in my written testimony. I'm happy to answer questions about it.

But the results of it as set forth in the ODNI report from this month are clear. The results of it are, first, confirmed reengagement. Seven out of 144—that's 4.9 percent. Suspected, 12 out of 144. That's 8.3 percent. Those are what the numbers are, sir, for this administration.

I'd point out also that with respect to the standards that are applied in defining what it even means to be confirmed or suspected it's important to point out, first, that confirmed is a preponderance of information standard. So this is not a reasonable doubt. This is not that we are——

Chairman ROYCE. The gentleman's time has expired.

If I could just go to the gentleman from Florida, Mr. Yoho, for his questions and then maybe a question from Mr. Trott and Mr. Connolly.

Mr. YOHO. I have more of a statement, and I appreciate it.

You know, to start with, when we speak about closing Guantanamo I'm glad to hear you on the record backing up what the administration said that they will not transfer the naval base back to Cuba.

We're talking about the detention center only. There are two entities there, as we're all aware of. As far as a recruiting tool, the Guantanamo Bay as a recruiting tool, I don't see how—I think that's a weak argument. Because if those people come to the United States is that not a recruiting tool, too?

So to say that they're in Guantanamo is going to be a stronger recruiting tool I think is sophistry at its finest because the jihadis are going to look at them being here in the belly of the great Satan.

So I think that argument is very weak and we shouldn't even talk about that. And I disagree with your comments about the Uruguay Six. I just came back there and met with their foreign minister.

They don't have a clue of what that negotiation was when it was negotiated under President Mujica. They don't know what the deals were, what the conditions were. They don't have a clue of monitoring and I think it's a joke.

But saying that, I think the overall success rate—if there were 780 total detainees we're down to 94 percent have been processed. That leaves only 6 percent, and of those 6 percent there's—that's taking out the 36 percent or the 36 that have already been cleared.

Yet this administration hasn't found them a suitable place to go and I would encourage you to move a little bit quicker on that.

And of the remaining 52 percent, if we take the 30 percent that we know will go into combat against our young men and women or suspected, that comes out to be 15.6 terrorists back fighting our young men and women and I don't think any American would want that or people around the world.

And I'm going to yield back the rest of my time back to Mr. Trott, if that's——

Chairman ROYCE. Yes, we're going to have one question from Mr. Trott and one question from Mr. Connolly.

Mr. TROTT. So thank you. I thank the gentleman from Florida.

So if we move the detainees to U.S. soil that's not going to be used as a recruitment tool by ISIS? They're going to go silent now that we've done right by our allies?

Mr. LEWIS. It still will be a tool but we take away—from a legal point of view we're taking away the issue that our allies are asking us to do. They're saying close Gitmo. So——

Mr. TROTT. And do you think our allies might change their position in light of Brussels and Paris, like was suggested earlier? Isn't there a chance—would you agree that there's a chance they will change their position with respect to our activities in Gitmo in light of recent events?

Mr. LEWIS. Sir, it's been a continuing position that they want Gitmo closed, that our leadership and the Bush administration leadership said that the costs of Gitmo outweigh the benefits.

Chairman ROYCE. Thank you, Mr. Trott.

Now we go to Mr. Connolly for his question.

Mr. CONNOLLY. Mr. Wolosky or Mr. Lewis, do you remember the CIA terrorist incident a number of years ago in Fairfax County?

Mr. LEWIS. Yes, sir.

Mr. CONNOLLY. Was the perpetrator of that terrorist incident caught and tried?

Mr. LEWIS. It's my understanding yes.

Mr. CONNOLLY. Was he tried in Guantanamo or was he tried in a U.S. district court right here in Virginia?

Mr. LEWIS. It's my understanding a U.S. district court here in Virginia.

Mr. CONNOLLY. And was he sentenced?

Mr. LEWIS. It's my understanding yes, sir.

Mr. CONNOLLY. He received the death sentence, as a matter of fact, did he not?

Mr. LEWIS. That I do not know personally. I know it was a severe sentence.

Mr. CONNOLLY. Yes, and somehow our system of justice worked. Not on Cuban soil—on Virginian soil. We could handle a terrorist and did.

I just—for the record, you know, we have to take into account the consequences of the symbolism of Guantanamo and, frankly, the fact that the suggestion is planted that we're not all that confident in our system of justice in handling terrorist cases and the fact of the matter is we do have experience and our system worked.

Thank you, Mr. Chairman.

Chairman ROYCE. Thank you, Mr. Connolly.

We have votes on the floor. We appreciate the time of our witnesses this morning, and our witnesses have agreed to meet with us in April in closed session so we appreciate that.

As you have heard, there are many concerns with the President's plan, especially given the ever-growing terrorist threat as evidenced by what happened in Brussels this week.

The points made by Mr. Trott and by Mr. Yoho bring to mind a conversation I had yesterday with the former NSA and CIA director about the concept that if you move them to U.S. soil, that in fact that will be a magnet for terrorists—the fact that jihadists are being held in the United States.

And so I think the last questions raised were also questions worth contemplating. But we will adjourn at this time for the votes and we thank our panel.

Mr. LEWIS. Thank you very much.

[Whereupon, at 10:54 p.m., the committee was adjourned.]

APPENDIX

MATERIAL SUBMITTED FOR THE RECORD

FULL COMMITTEE HEARING NOTICE
COMMITTEE ON FOREIGN AFFAIRS
U.S. HOUSE OF REPRESENTATIVES
WASHINGTON, DC 20515-6128

Edward R. Royce (R-CA), Chairman

March 23, 2016

TO: MEMBERS OF THE COMMITTEE ON FOREIGN AFFAIRS

You are respectfully requested to attend an OPEN hearing of the Committee on Foreign Affairs, to be held in Room 2172 of the Rayburn House Office Building (and available live on the Committee website at http://www.ForeignAffairs.house.gov):

DATE: Wednesday, March 23, 2016

TIME: 9:30 a.m.

SUBJECT: The Administration's Plan to Close the Guantanamo Bay Detention Facility: At What Foreign Policy and National Security Cost?

WITNESSES: Mr. Lee Wolosky
Special Envoy for Guantanamo Closure
U.S. Department of State

Mr. Paul M. Lewis
Special Envoy for Guantanamo Detention Closure
U.S. Department of Defense

By Direction of the Chairman

The Committee on Foreign Affairs seeks to make its facilities accessible to persons with disabilities. If you are in need of special accommodations, please call 202/225-5021 at least four business days in advance of the event, whenever practicable. Questions with regard to special accommodations in general (including availability of Committee materials in alternative formats and assistive listening devices) may be directed to the Committee.

COMMITTEE ON FOREIGN AFFAIRS
MINUTES OF FULL COMMITTEE HEARING

Day __Wednesday__ Date ___3/23/2016___ Room ____2172____

Starting Time ___9:32___ Ending Time ___10:54___

Recesses | _0_ | (____to ____) (____to ____) (____to ____) (____to ____) (____to ____) (to ___)

Presiding Member(s)

Chairman Edward R. Royce

Check all of the following that apply:

Open Session ☑
Executive (closed) Session ☐
Televised ☑

Electronically Recorded (taped) ☑
Stenographic Record ☑

TITLE OF HEARING:

The Administration's Plan to Close the Guantanamo Bay Detention Facility: At What Foreign Policy and National Security Cost?

COMMITTEE MEMBERS PRESENT:

See attached.

NON-COMMITTEE MEMBERS PRESENT:

none

HEARING WITNESSES: Same as meeting notice attached? Yes ☑ **No** ☐
(If "no", please list below and include title, agency, department, or organization.)

STATEMENTS FOR THE RECORD: _(List any statements submitted for the record.)_

IFR - Rep. Eliot Engel
SFR - Rep. Jeff Duncan
QFR - Chairman Edward Royce

TIME SCHEDULED TO RECONVENE _____
or
TIME ADJOURNED _10:54_

Jean Marter, Director of Committee Operations

52

HOUSE COMMITTEE ON FOREIGN AFFAIRS
FULL COMMITTEE HEARING

PRESENT	MEMBER
X	Edward R. Royce, CA
X	Christopher H. Smith, NJ
X	Ileana Ros-Lehtinen, FL
X	Dana Rohrabacher, CA
	Steve Chabot, OH
	Joe Wilson, SC
	Michael T. McCaul, TX
X	Ted Poe, TX
X	Matt Salmon, AZ
X	Darrell Issa, CA
	Tom Marino, PA
X	Jeff Duncan, SC
X	Mo Brooks, AL
	Paul Cook, CA
X	Randy Weber, TX
	Scott Perry, PA
	Ron DeSantis, FL
	Mark Meadows, NC
X	Ted Yoho, FL
	Curt Clawson, FL
	Scott DesJarlais, TN
X	Reid Ribble, WI
X	Dave Trott, MI
X	Lee Zeldin, NY
	Dan Donovan, NY

PRESENT	MEMBER
X	Eliot L. Engel, NY
	Brad Sherman, CA
X	Gregory W. Meeks, NY
	Albio Sires, NJ
X	Gerald E. Connolly, VA
X	Theodore E. Deutch, FL
	Brian Higgins, NY
	Karen Bass, CA
X	William Keating, MA
X	David Cicilline, RI
	Alan Grayson, FL
X	Ami Bera, CA
X	Alan S. Lowenthal, CA
	Grace Meng, NY
	Lois Frankel, FL
	Tulsi Gabbard, HI
	Joaquin Castro, TX
X	Robin Kelly, IL
	Brendan Boyle, PA

Congressman Jeff Duncan – Statement for the Record
3/23/16 HFAC Hearing: The Administration's Plan to Close the Guantanamo Bay
Detention Facility: At What Foreign Policy and National Security Cost?

Mr. Chairman, I want to thank you for holding this incredibly important hearing on the President's plan to close the detention facility at Guantanamo Bay, Cuba. I believe that this decision is one that is a detriment to our foreign policy and national security.

Guantanamo Bay is a United States national security asset. Closing the facility would once again demonstrate how this President is more concerned with his political agenda than the safety and security of this nation and the will of the American people.

Instead of listening to the will of the American people and Congress, President Obama wants to close the detention facility at Guantanamo Bay and house some of the remaining detainees within the United States. Currently, that is prohibited. Attorney General Lynch confirmed multiple times that doing so is expressly against the law. The Department of Defense cannot use any appropriated funds to bring prisoners to the U.S. However, the Defense Department has already surveyed multiple sites within the U.S. to house these prisoners. One of those sites being the Naval Brig in Charleston, South Carolina. I can tell you without a doubt that the people of South Carolina do not want terrorists brought to their state. Our governor does not want these terrorists brought to the state. In fact, Governor Haley sent a letter to Defense Secretary Carter stating that she strongly opposed the transfer of terrorists to South Carolina. Yet, instead of consulting with state governors and listening to the people, this Administration is making plans to move ahead with the closure of the facility and the transfer of prisoners to the United States.

Furthermore, as part of his closure plan, the President wants to transfer 35 of the remaining 91 detainees to other countries. What assurances do we as Members of Congress and American citizens have that those terrorists released will not rejoin terrorist groups? According to Secretary Kerry, they're just "not supposed to" reengage in terrorist activity. That's our policy? We're just hoping for the best when it comes to the safety and security of our country? That is not an effective national security strategy. That fact is we don't have any assurances that those released will not reengage in terrorist activity. According to a report that the Office of the Director of National Intelligence released in January of 2016, 17.5% of the detainees released are confirmed of reengaging in terrorist activity. 12.7% are suspected of reengaging. That is over 30% that have reengaged when we're just hoping that they don't. Most recently, in February of this year, a former Guantanamo Bay detainee was arrested in Spain for ties to ISIS. Additionally, we know that Americans have died because of detainees being released from Guantanamo Bay. When these terrorists are housed at Guantanamo Bay, Cuba, we can ensure that they are in a secure location, isolated from American citizens and isolated from other terrorist groups. This is not a smart national security strategy to close the facility, and it only endangers the lives of Americans.

The White House claims that the President will not return Guantanamo Bay to Cuba, although Raul Castro says that returning Guantanamo Bay is a prerequisite to normalizing relations. However, when it comes to these decisions, how can we trust this Administration? Looking back to other foreign policy and nation security decisions this President has made, it is clear that he is more concerned with advancing his own legacy rather than safety and security. Senior Iranian officials say that the President began talks with them in 2009, unbeknownst to Members of Congress. These negotiations only led to a deal where the U.S. made concessions to

54

Iran—a state sponsor of terror—rather than the other way around. Additionally, President Obama moved ahead with normalizing relations with Cuba—a state sponsor of terror as well—without bringing in Congress and without negotiating terms that would benefit the Cuban dissidents being oppressed by the Castro regime. President Obama is not concerned about Cuban dissidents and how this normalization will affect them. Rather, once again, he is more concerned with checking boxes off his agenda than putting the national security of our country first.

The United States Naval Station at Guantanamo Bay, Cuba, is the only U.S. military main operating base in the Caribbean. It is a unique and strategic enabler for the U.S. government to ensure regional security objectives are met. Closing the detention facility at Guantanamo Bay would only be hindering our military's effectiveness in protecting U.S. citizens. I implore the President to listen to the American people and Members of Congress and keep the detention facility open.

MATERIAL SUBMITTED FOR THE RECORD BY THE HONORABLE ELIOT L. ENGEL, A
REPRESENTATIVE IN CONGRESS FROM THE STATE OF NEW YORK

Statement for the Record
House Foreign Affairs Committee Hearing – March 23, 2016

STATEMENT FOR THE RECORD OF
MAJOR GENERAL MICHAEL R. LEHNERT, USMC (RET.)
BEFORE THE
HOUSE ARMED SERVICED COMMITTEE
MARCH 23, 2016

THE NEED TO SHUTTER THE DETENTION FACILITY AT GUANTANAMO BAY, CUBA

Chairman Royce, Ranking Member Engel, Members of the Committee, thank you for the opportunity to share my views with you.

The goal of terrorism is to change behavior and to make us live in fear. On 9/11 America changed.

In September 2001 I was a new brigadier general at Camp Lejeune, North Carolina commanding an 8,000 man force of Marines and Sailors. America made the decision to go to war in Afghanistan, and some of my troops were deployed early into the fight. And as we began to take captives, the question of what to do with them became more imperative. Many in the Administration believed that these individuals represented an intelligence treasure trove.

The decision to send me and my command to Guantanamo employed a strange logic. Guantanamo has been used for decades by Administrations from both parties as an extra-legal zone to buy time during crises. It had been the site for several Cuban and Haitian migrant camps and in fact I'd commanded the Guantanamo camps in 1995 during the Clinton era when we had 18,000 Cubans and Haitians there on the ground. Though the U.S. Army is doctrinally responsible for prisoner of war camps, the Marines ability to deploy rapidly coupled with my past experience probably drove the initial decision. That there is a vast difference between an economic migrant and a prisoner of war seemed lost on the policy makers in Washington.

So in early January 2002 I received a deployment order to form a Joint Task Force, get to Cuba and build the first 100 cells in 96 hours and be prepared to receive prisoners of war (that's what we called them then). That we created a detention facility in 87 hours said a great deal about the young troops I led but it also drove a series of unfortunate early decisions. Many of those Administration decisions involved the application of both U.S. and International law. I'm not a lawyer but it is very clear that when we decided to forgo generations of legal precedent and start all over, bad things happen.

As enemy prisoners of war began to arrive, even their titles began to change. They were not enemy combatants. I was told that I was to "be guided by but not required to follow the Geneva Conventions." When I asked my lawyers what that meant, I was told "pretty much whatever they want it to mean." Though we were told that these were "worst of the worst" many detainees appeared to have been sent based upon their need for medical or psychiatric attention. Some had poor excuses for being caught in a war zone and many were there because we were paying bounties for terrorists. We did not understand the Afghan tribal system. For a tribal leader what better way to enrich yourself while resolving old grudges than to finger a neighbor who was your enemy regardless of his support for either al Qaeda or the Taliban?

Statement for the Record
House Foreign Affairs Committee Hearing – March 23, 2016

It took time to recognize our early storing process was flawed. Almost all who arrived said they were simply "studying in a madrassa." Some were students. Others were truly enemy combatants. Our failure to apply Article V hearings at the point of capture as required by the Geneva Conventions was beginning to result in detainees being sent who shouldn't have been sent.

I'd been sent down for 60 days with instructions to turn the command over to the Army once they were able to get down to GTMO. I was there nearly 100 days when I was finally relieved. By this time, it was becoming more apparent that GTMO was housing a number of prisoners who were either noncombatants or simply low level fighters.

Perhaps the best proof that we sent the wrong people to Guantanamo is that of the 780 who have ever been in Guantanamo, 647 were released back to their country of origin or resettled without action.

So why should be close Guantanamo?

First and foremost because Guantanamo's continued existence hurts us in our prosecution of the fight against terrorists. It feeds into the narrative that the United States is not a nation of laws nor one that respects human rights. Military commissions create a façade of justice. There are currently only three detainees at Guantanamo who were convicted by military commissions though they have been in operation for over eight years. Four previous convictions by commissions were overturned by the U.S. Supreme Court. U.S. Federal Courts have been much more successful in getting convictions of terrorists, and those convictions have held up under appeal. Our reliance upon military commissions, the absence of precedent, and their inability to resolve these cases make a mockery of our claim that we are a nation of laws.

Secondly, Guantanamo's extra-legal status is inconsistent with our values as Americans. When I was first commissioned and every subsequent promotion thereafter I took the oath of office to support and defend the Constitution of the United States. Unlike the enlisted oath, officers don't swear allegiance to the President or to their chain of command. The authors of the officers' oath knew exactly what they were doing. They recognized that the Constitution is the seminal document that governs who we are as a people and that commissioned officers must have the wisdom to align their actions to the Constitution. To have a place on earth where the Constitution does not apply is simply un-American. It also begs the question that if it means nothing in Guantanamo, does our Constitution and the requirement to live by it stop at the water's edge? When we fail to live by that remarkable document it diminishes us as a people.

Thirdly, Guantanamo and all locations where so-called enhanced interrogation techniques were practiced are a blight on our honor and put our citizens at greater risk. It's no accident that many captives executed by terrorists were filmed being killed wearing orange jump suits. We are feeding the terrorist narrative not creating our own. Torture and its euphemism "enhanced interrogation techniques" don't make us safer. They don't deliver useful intelligence, and these practices are beneath us. When Senator McCain stood on the floor of the Senate on December 9, 2014, and delivered his opposition to torture, it was his finest hour in a lifetime of service. Despite significant pushback from many in his own party, he is the one elected member of our government with absolute credibility on this topic. Torture is wrong. It is also ineffective. Guantanamo is a symbol of a flawed, ill-considered and shameful policy. It must be closed.

Statement for the Record
House Foreign Affairs Committee Hearing – March 23, 2016

Guantanamo was a mistake. History will reflect that. It was created in the early days as a consequence of fear, anger, and political expediency. It ignored centuries of rule of law and international agreements. It does not make us safer, and it sullies who we are as a nation. That in over a decade we have failed to acknowledge the mistake and change course is unforgivable and ignorant.

We can win the fight against terrorism and religious extremism, but only if we adhere to our American values. If we kill every terrorist on the planet but in the process abandon the Constitution and our values, then in their deaths they will have succeeded, and we will no longer be Americans and this country will no longer be the bastion of democracy, freedom, and liberty.

Terrorists want to make us live in fear. They want to change who we are as a people. By both standards as long as Guantanamo continues, they are winning, and we are playing into their hands.

Thank you for the opportunity to share my views with you.

CHARRTS No.: HFAC-01-001
Hearing Date: March 23, 2016
Committee: HFAC
Member: Congressman Royce
Witness: Mr. Lewis

Closure and Transfer Plan

Question: Which facilities inside the continental United States has the Administration examined for purposes of relocating Guantanamo detainees?

Answer:
The Administration's plan for closing the detention facility at Guantanamo Bay does not endorse a specific facility in the United States to house detainees who cannot be transferred to foreign countries. Rather, the plan describes a prototype for a U.S. detention facility in the United States, based on careful work over the last several months and past reviews by the Department of Defense.

In 2015, a Department of Defense team carried out a review of military, Federal, and state facilities that could be modified to securely and humanely hold detainees transferred from Guantanamo Bay and to serve as a military commissions site. Site visits were conducted to develop estimated costs. The 2015 team visited: U.S. Disciplinary Barracks and Midwest Joint Regional Correction Facility in Fort Leavenworth, Kansas; Naval Consolidated Brig at Joint Base Charleston, South Carolina; Colorado State Penitentiary II in Canon City, Colorado; and the Federal Correctional Institute in Florence, Colorado. In past reviews, the Department of Defense also visited sites in Illinois and Michigan.

Question: Which cities and states inside the continental United States has the Administration considered for purposes of constructing new facilities to house Guantanamo detainees?

Answer:
To build an estimate for detention in the United States in the closure plan, the Department of Defense relied on surveys of facilities conducted in 2009, 2012, and 2015. This data was used to estimate costs for prototypes of detention facilities; no site has been selected. The 2015 team visited: U.S. Disciplinary Barracks and Midwest Joint Regional Correction Facility in Fort Leavenworth, Kansas; Naval Consolidated Brig at Joint Base Charleston, South Carolina; Colorado State Penitentiary II in Canon City, Colorado; and the Federal Correctional Institute in Florence, Colorado. The estimate also relied on past reviews of facilities, in Illinois and Michigan. Rather than initiate a debate about the merits of any particular location, the Administration seeks a dialogue with Congress and to establish parameters for a U.S. detention facility before reaching any conclusions.

Question: Has the Administration notified communities that they are being considered as potential new sites? To what extent has the Administration engaged with state and local leaders, including surrounding cities and neighborhoods? What is their reaction? If there has been no engagement, why not?

Answer:

No location has been proposed or selected. Prior to visits in 2015, the Administration notified congressional delegations and local officials, no additional outreach has taken place. The Administration seeks a dialogue with Congress and to establish parameters for a U.S. detention facility before reaching any conclusions.

Question: The projected cost savings contained in the February 23, 2016, closure plan depend on the release of an additional 35 detainees. How did the Defense Department arrive at this number? If those detainees were not transferred, would the plan still be cost effective? Did the review board approve the transfer of these individuals before or after it was determined that 35 would make the plan cost effective?

Answer:

Each of the U.S. locations is more cost effective than the continued use of the detention facilities at Guantanamo, no matter the number of detainees being held there. At the time the plan was submitted, there were 35 detainees eligible for transfer, as determined by either the 2009 Executive Order or the Periodic Review Board.

Question: Did the Administration assess the costs and risks to the 13 communities that surround these facilities or just the federal cost? How about the state and local costs associated with these facilities? If not, is that because the Administration determined that there were no risks or costs to the affected communities and states?

Answer:

The Department of Defense estimated detention facility refurbishment and construction costs based on sites surveyed in 2009, 2012, and 2015 and from data on Bureau of Prisons and Department of Defense correctional facilities construction costs. The plan describes three prototypes drawing on a variety of data, including design and cost data for Department of Defense correction facilitates and information gathered during surveys. Locality costs require additional analysis; however, statutory restrictions prevented the Department of Defense from conducting in-depth planning and design that would be necessary to develop budget-quality estimates for individual sites.

Question: If state and local costs are not already included in the closure plan, how would the cost projections change?

Answer:

State and local costs can only be determined once a location is chosen and a more comprehensive site survey for that location is conducted. Statutory restrictions prevented the Department of Defense from conducting this kind of in-depth planning.

Question: Reflecting on the transfer of detainees from Guantanamo to foreign countries made to date, how long does it take from the time a transfer is ordered to be carried out until the detainee is on board military aircraft and underway?

Answer:
In accordance with current statutory requirements, the Secretary of Defense certifies to the appropriate committees of Congress his decision to transfer a detainee at least 30 days before the transfer occurs. Transfers normally occur shortly after the 30 day statutory waiting period has expired.

Question: If the detention facility at Guantanamo were to close, what would the Defense Department do with the site and fixtures?

Answer:
To the extent that is feasible, the Department plans to use remaining facilities to support other enduring missions at Guantanamo.

Question: Aside from location and potential costs, what would be different about a new or modified facility inside the continental United States? Please be specific.

Answer:
A new or modified facility inside the continental United States would allow for detention and support facilities to be more closely collocated, creating both manpower and cost efficiencies in the detention operation. As detainees age, it would allow access to medical facilities and specialists not available at Guantanamo.

The facility would continue to provide secure, humane detention based on U.S. law and international commitments.

Americans Killed by Released Detainees

Question: Mr. Paul Lewis testified that, "unfortunately, there have been Americans that have died because of Gitmo detainees" released from Guantanamo Bay. Please provide details. How many Americans have died? When, where, and how were they killed? Which detainee was responsible? When were they released and where were they transferred? Did the host country fail to adhere to its commitments under the transfer agreement?

Answer:
Our understanding is less than 15 of the nearly 700 former Guantanamo detainees have participated in attacks against Americans or Coalition Forces. All of these attacks occurred in Afghanistan. Each of these detainees was transferred from Guantanamo before 2009, and we believe that eight of them are either dead or in foreign government custody. Because many of these incidents were large-scale firefights in a war zone, we cannot always distinguish whether Americans were killed by the former detainees vice other participants. This is all that the Department can share in an unclassified setting. I defer to the Intelligence Community to provide additional information in a classified setting.

www.ingramcontent.com/pod-product-compliance
Lightning Source LLC
Chambersburg PA
CBHW081856280526
45789CB00007B/2728